The Governance of Regulators

Driving Performance at Peru's Energy and Mining Regulator

Please cite this publication as:
OECD (2019), *Driving Performance at Peru's Energy and Mining Regulator*, The Governance of Regulators, OECD Publishing, Paris.
https://doi.org/10.1787/9789264310865-en

ISBN 978-92-64-31085-8 (print)
ISBN 978-92-64-31086-5 (pdf)

The Governance of Regulators
ISSN 2415-1432 (print)
ISSN 2415-1440 (online)

Photo credits: Cover © Leigh Prather - Fotolia.com, © Mr.Vander - Fotolia.com, © magann - Fotolia.com.

Corrigenda to OECD publications may be found on line at: *www.oecd.org/about/publishing/corrigenda.htm*.

Foreword

Economic regulators should play an important role as impartial referees to guarantee the predictability and certainty of regulatory regimes – crucial features for attracting investment. Their job is inherently a complex one, requiring neutral engagement with a variety of actors, including government, citizens and consumers, and operators. The model of independent economic regulation, based on strong technical capacity, transparency, autonomy and constructive engagement with stakeholders, can help regulators tackle this complex landscape. Moreover, independent regulators can provide certainty to markets and society during periods of external instability. However, regulators need to be correctly equipped to carry out these fundamental tasks and stay abreast of market evolutions.

To support regulators as they face these challenges, the OECD has developed a framework to assess and strengthen their organisational performance and governance structures. The framework analyses regulators' internal and external governance, including their organisational structures, behaviour, accountability, business processes, reporting and performance management, as well as role clarity, relationships, distribution of powers and responsibilities with other government and non-government stakeholders.

This report applies this OECD framework to Osinergmin, the Peruvian regulator responsible for energy markets and large and medium mines. The review finds that Osinergmin has achieved a strong reputation as an autonomous and technically competent regulator. The regulator has evolved by absorbing new functions and changing its competencies over the last 20 years.

While this review considers that Osinergmin has adapted with a relatively high degree of success to meet its changing mandate since 1997, it is also facing a number of challenges. Most importantly, it should build on its technical competency and strive to become a more proactive organisation with clearer objectives for the regulated sectors and a stable institutional role.

The report provides recommendations to help Osinergmin face this key challenge. These recommendations are intended to complement the Osinergmin's ongoing efforts to improve its governance processes in line with best practices. The review underlines, amongst others, the importance of co-ordinating with other agencies more formally and regularly, better communicating the impacts of austerity and fiscal measures, and building stronger consultation practices to strengthen stakeholder engagement.

These actions, among others put forward in this report, could help Osinergmin build on its technical work and reputation to become an example of institutional maturity within the Peruvian public administration.

Finally, the review, carried out in parallel with that of the Peru's telecommunications regulator, OSIPTEL, recommends that Peru's four economic regulators work together more effectively to share best practices and address common challenges.

This report is part of the OECD work programme on the governance of regulators and regulatory policy, led by the OECD Network of Economic Regulators and the OECD Regulatory Policy Committee with the support of the Regulatory Policy Division of the OECD Directorate of Public Governance. The Directorate's mission is to help government at all levels design and implement strategic, evidence-based and innovative policies that support sustainable economic and social development.

Acknowledgements

This report was co-ordinated and prepared by Lorenzo Casullo, James Drummond and Andrea Pérez under the guidance of Anna Pietikainen. The work underlying the report was led by Filippo Cavassini. Substantive comments were provided by Anna Pietikainen, Filippo Cavassini, Shelly Hsieh and Nick Malyshev, Head of the Regulatory Policy Division. The work received the encouragement and support of Marcos Bonturi, Director, and Irène Hors, Deputy Director, Public Governance Directorate. Jennifer Stein co-ordinated the editorial process and Kate Lancaster and Andrea Uhrhammer provided editorial support. Alejandro Camacho of the OECD Mexico Centre provided support for the translation of the report into Spanish, which was prepared by Solar Servicios Editoriales.

The team included three peer reviewers from the members of the OECD Network of Economic Regulators (NER), who participated in a policy mission to Peru and provided extensive inputs and feedback throughout the development of the review: Ms. Cristina Cifuentes, Commissioner, Australian Competition and Consumer Commission (ACCC), Australia; Mr. Sergio Pimentel, Commissioner, National Hydrocarbons Commission (CNH), Mexico; and Ms. Ana Albuquerque, Member of the Executive Board, Water Regulatory Authority (ERSAR), Portugal.

The report would not have been possible without the support of Osinergmin and its staff. The team would in particular like to thank the following colleagues for their unique assistance in collecting data and information, organising the team's missions to Peru and providing feedback at different stages of the development of the review: Daniel Schmerler, President of the Board of Directors; José Carlos Velarde, General Manager; Abel Rodriguez, Head of the Policy and Economic Analysis Department; Victor Raul Zurita Saldaña, Senior Specialist – Policy and Economic Analysis Department; Darha Chávez Vásquez, Assistant – Policy and Economic Analysis Department; and Ksenia Gutsol, Fulbright Public Policy Fellow. Interviews and comments from various government, industry and public stakeholders during the review process also contributed to the analysis presented in the report.

A draft of the report was discussed at the OECD Network of Economic Regulators in November 2018.

Table of contents

Tables

Figures

Boxes

Acronyms and abbreviations

ACCC	Australian Competition and Consumer Commission
AGCOM	The Italian telecommunications regulator (*Autorità per le garanzie nelle comunicazioni*)
ARIAE	Energy Regulators Iberoamerican Association (*Asociación Iberoamericana de Entidades Reguladoras de la Energía*)
ASEA	Safety, Energy and Environment Agency (*Agencia de Seguridad, Energía y Ambiente de México*).
CEPLAN	National Centre for Strategic Planning (*Centro Nacional de Planeamiento estratégico*)
CGR	Comptroller General of the Republic of Peru (*Contraloría General de la República del Perú*)
CNG	Compressed Natural Gas
CNH	National Hydrocarbons Commission (*Comisión Nacional de Hidrocarburos de México).*
COES	Economic Operating Committee of the National Interconnected System (*Comité de Operación Económica del Sistema Interconectado Nacional*)
CODECO	Commission for Consumer Defence and Regulators of Public Utilities (*Comisión Defensa del Consumidor y Organismos Reguladores de los Servicios Públicos*)
CPP	Peruvian Political Constitution (*Constitución Política del Perú*)
CRE	Energy Regulatory Comission *(Comisión Reguladora de Energía de México*)
CTE	Electricity Tariffs Commission (*Comisión de Tarifas de Electricidad*)
DAV	Distribution Added Value (*Valor Agregado de Distribución*)
DREM	Regional Directorates of Energy and Mines (*Direcciones Regionales de Energía y Minas*)
EPERS	Perception Surveys of Regulated and Supervised Companies (*Encuesta de Percepción a Empresas Reguladas y Supervisadas*)
ERSAR	Portuguese Water and Waste Services Regulation Authority
FISE	The Energy Social Inclusion Fund (*Fondo de Inclusión Social Energético*)
FOSE	Osinergmin's Electric Social Compensation Fund (*Fondo de Compensación Social Eléctrica*)
GAJ	Legal Advice Department (*Gerencia Asesoría Jurídica*)
GART	Adjunct Department of tariff regulation (Gerencia Adjunta de Regulación Tarifaria)
GFE	Electrical Audit Department (*Gerencia de Fiscalización Eléctrica*)

GFGN	Natural Gas Audit Department (*Gerencia de Fiscalización de Gas Natural*)
GFHL	Liquid Hydrocarbons Audit Department (*Gerencia de Fiscalización de Hidrocarburos Líquidos*)
GFM	Mineral Audit Department (*Gerencia de Fiscalización Minera*)
GG	General Manager (*Gerente General*)
GPAE	Policy and Economic Research Department (Gerencia de Políticas y Análisis Económico)
GPPM	Planning, Budget and Modernisation Department (*Gerencia de Planeamiento, Presupuesto y Modernización*)
GTH	Human Talent Management (*Gerencia de Talento Humano*)
ICER	International Confederation of Energy Regulators (*Confederación Internacional de Reguladores de Energía*)
INACAL	National Institute of Quality (*Instituto Nacional de Calidad*)
Indecopi	National Institute for the Defense of Competition and Intellectual Property (*Instituto Nacional de Defensa de la Competencia y Protección de la Propiedad Intelectual*)
ISO	International Organisation for Standardisation
JARU	Appeals Board of User Claims (*Junta de Apelaciones de Reclamos de Usuarios*)
LMOR	Framework Law on Regulatory Agencies for Private Investment in Public Utilities (*Ley Marco de los Organismos Reguladores de la Inversión Privada en los Servicios Públicos*)
LOGR	Organic Law of Regional Governments (*Ley Orgánica de Gobiernos Regionales*)
LOM	Organic Law of Municipalities (*Ley Orgánica de Municipalidades*)
LOPE	Organic Law of the Executive Power (*Ley Orgánica del Poder Ejecutivo*)
LNG	Liquefied Natural Gas
LPG	Liquefied Petroleum Gas
MEF	Ministry of Economy and Finance (*Ministerio de Economía y Finanzas*)
MEM	Ministry of Energy and Mines (*Ministerio de Energía y Minas*)
MGPP	Processes and Procedures Manual and Procedures (*Manual de Gestión de Procesos y Procedimientos*)
MINCETUR	Ministry of External Trade and Tourism (*Ministerio de Comercio Exterior y Turismo*)
MINJUS	Ministry of Justice and Human Rights (*Ministerio de Justicia y Derechos Humanos*)
MOF	Organisational and Functions Manual (*Manual de Organización y Funciones*)
MW	Mega watts
NEB	National Energy Board of Canada
NER	Network of Economic Regulators
PAFER	Performance Assessment Framework for Economic Regulators
PCM	Presidency of the Council of Ministers (*Presidencia del Consejo de Ministros*)
PEDN	National Strategic Development Plan (*Plan Estratégico de Desarrollo Nacional*)

PEI	Strategic Institutional Plan (*Plan Estratégico Institucional*)
POI	Operational Institutional Plan (*Objetivos Estratégicos Institucionales*)
PPP	Public Private Partnerships
ProInversión	Agency for the Promotion of Investment (*Agencia de Promoción de la Inversión Privada*)
OAF	Administration and Finance Department (*Oficina de Administración y Finanzas*)
OC	Communications Department (*Oficina de Comunicaciones*)
OECD	Organisation for Economic Co-operation and Development
OEFA	Agency for Environmental Assessment and Control (*Organismo de Evaluación y Fiscalización Ambiental*)
OEM	Energy and Mining Observatory (*Observatorio Energético Minero*)
OCI	Institutional Control Body (*Órgano de Control Institucional*)
OPC	Planning and Control of Management Department (*Oficina de Planeamiento y Control*)
OSINERG	Organism for the Investment in Energy (*Organismo Supervisor de Inversión en Energía*)
Osinergmin	Supervisory Agency for Investment in Energy and Mining (*Organismo Supervisor de la Inversión en Energía y Minería*)
OSIPTEL	Supervisory Agency for Private Investment in Telecommunications (*Organismo Suupervisor de Inversión Privada en Telecomunicaciones*)
OSITRAN	Supervisory Agency for Investment in Public Transport Infrastructure (*Organismo Supervisor de la Inversión en Infraestructura de Transporte de Uso Público*)
RER	Renewable Energy Resources
RIA	Regulatory Impact Assessment
RQA	Regulatory Quality Assessment
SAIDI	System Average Interruption Duration Index
SAIFI	System Average Interruption Frequency Index
SERVIR	National Civil Service Authority (*Autoridad Nacional del Servicio Civil*)
SINAPLAN	National System of Strategic Planning (*Sistema Nacional de Planeamiento Estratégico*)
SUNASS	National Superintendence of Sanitation Services (*Superintendencia Nacional de Servicios de Saneamiento*)
SUNAFIL	National Superintendency of Labor Inspection (*Superintendencia Nacional de Fiscalización Laboral*)
SUNAT	National Superintendency of Customs and Tax Administration (Superintendencia Nacional de Administración Tributaria).
TASTEM	Administrative Tribunal of Energy and Mines Sanctions (*Tribunal de Apelaciones de Sanciones en Temas de Energía y Minería*)
TSC	Controversies Settlement Court (*Tribunal de Solución de Controversias*)

Executive summary

Osinergmin (*Organismo Supervisor de la Inversión en Energía y Minería*) was created in 1997 as Peru's safety and economic regulator for energy and mining infrastructure. The regulator has gained a strong reputation as an autonomous and technically competent regulator over the last 20 years, overseeing sectors of strategic importance to Peru in terms of economic development, investment attraction and export performance. A key challenge for Osinergmin is to build on its technical competency and autonomy and strive for greater institutional maturity in a complex governance system.

Role and objectives

Osinergmin is a specialised and decentralised regulatory body with technical, administrative, economic and financial autonomy. Like all Peruvian regulators, it relies on the Presidency of the Council of Ministers (PCM) for approval for several procedures and is subject to public finance rules.

Osinergmin's role, mandate and structure have changed over the past 20 years, absorbing new powers (e.g. mining sector supervision, administration of the Energy Social Inclusion Fund) and losing others (e.g. supervising compliance with environmental and labour standards). In the absence of formal co-ordination structures, a complex governance system for the sector has emerged.

Osinergmin sets out a Strategic Institutional Plan (PEI) underpinned by the values of commitment, excellence, service, integrity and autonomy. Osinergmin is active in communication and outreach activities to provide information about its work, especially important in light of changing roles and functions.

Key recommendations

- ***Develop*** specific instruments to ensure more structured and regular co-ordination among all public agencies involved in the supervision of the energy and mining sectors, as well as the electricity system operator.
- ***Carry out*** a mid-term evaluation of the PEI in order to prioritise objectives more systematically, develop a vision for the regulated sectors and more closely link budgeting and planning to forecast needs and minimise risks.

Input

Osinergmin is entirely funded by resources received from the regulated sectors. New public finance and austerity measures have placed limitations on budget execution and raised uncertainty around the regulator's ability to plan its resources and fulfil some of its activities.

All stakeholders recognise the competence of Osinergmin's staff, and staff report high levels of satisfaction and low turnover rates. Nevertheless, the presence of a dual employment framework and salary caps set by central government may reduce the regulator's attractiveness compared to the private sector in the long run.

Key recommendations

- ***Map*** the impacts of funding uncertainty on budget execution, seeking clarity from government and advocating for the principles of cost recovery and transparency to be key drivers of Osinergmin's funding model.
- ***Continue*** to attract and retain competent staff, regularly updating existing plans for maintaining technical expertise, monitoring salaries compared to the private sector and investing in recruitment strategies for new graduates.

Process

The Board of Directors, led by the President, is the decision-making body in Osinergmin. The Board meetings tend to focus on complex operational matters and only a limited amount of time is dedicated to strategic planning and longer-term thinking.

Osinergmin demonstrated institutional agility in adapting its mandate and functions. To complete this transition, further changes in internal organisation would be beneficial, although these require the government's approval.

Osinergmin has been a pioneer amongst Peruvian government agencies in implementing regulatory impact assessments (RIA) and *ex post* evaluations. The regulator also places a high priority on transparent and accountable decision making, though there is no effective forum for dialogue with regulated entities and users.

Enforcement and inspections of the safety of energy and mining infrastructure are core functions of Osinergmin, but the regulator carries those out with little co-ordination with other supervisory agencies (e.g. on reporting requirements for companies) and the large number of norms hamper the regulator's ability to manage effectively the volume and frequency of inspections.

Key recommendations

- ***Assess*** whether the activity and duties of the Board reflect its mandate and structure, encouraging Board members to focus more of their limited time on strategic matters.
- Starting from the existing Manual of Functions, ***clarify*** some internal functions (e.g. communications, regional activities), spread executive responsibilities more widely, promote accountability measures and establish formal mechanisms for quality control.
- ***Continue*** to invest in regulatory management tools and processes, including by strengthening processes for regular engagement and dialogue with stakeholders.
- ***Develop*** an Enforcement and Compliance Strategy with a view to establishing a closer working relationship with regulated entities and improving the efficiency of inspections activities.

Output and outcome

Osinergmin's strategic institutional plan for 2014-21 has a balance of input-related, process-related and output-related objectives. Five objectives are devoted to improving stakeholder relationships and an additional internal process indicator focuses on better communication with stakeholders, placing emphasis on the outward-facing aspects of the regulator's activity. However, the various performance measures collected by the regulator predominantly focus on internal management goals such as timeliness of projects and budget execution. Indicators on the quality of regulatory actions and stakeholders' perception are collected but not presently streamlined into the strategic framework.

Osinergmin reports on the performance of regulated entities, mainly at the national level, through a number of different channels, including its annual reports, quarterly newsletter and statistical reports. The online Energy and Mining Observatory represents a significant step forward in the provision of integrated, accessible data and analysis for the electricity, hydrocarbons and mining sectors.

Different reporting requirements result in a fragmented flow of information going from Osinergmin to the Executive and the Legislature.

Key recommendations

- ***Update*** a dashboard of performance measures aimed at enhancing the strategic focus of objectives and reducing the number of initiatives.
- ***Examine*** the quality of the regulator's actions in addition to their timeliness, both through internal and external perception surveys.
- ***Adopt*** a comprehensive approach to data management with improved interfaces with regulated entities, building on the Energy and Mining Observatory.
- ***Renew*** the regulator's focus on sub-national dynamics, including by strengthening the role of regional activities and publishing regional performance reports.
- ***Advocate*** for more structured reporting requirements to both the Executive and the Legislature.

Assessment and recommendations

Introduction

This assessment and recommendations chapter focuses on the external and internal governance arrangements of Peru's energy and mining infrastructure regulator (Osinergmin), and presents policy recommendations that aim to improve the performance of the regulator. The review finds that Osinergmin's key challenge is to build on widespread recognition of its technical competency and autonomy and strive for greater institutional maturity. This requires renewed attention to external governance arrangements, such as co-ordination mechanisms and greater accountability, aiming for constructive dialogue with all stakeholders. It also calls for internal organisational frameworks, management systems and capabilities to evolve so that Osinergmin can continue to tackle current and emerging challenges effectively. In doing so, the regulator will evolve from a reactive organisation, competently able to address emergencies and resolve crises, to a proactive institution with a vision for the energy and mining sectors and a relationship of trust with key stakeholders.

High-level message

Osinergmin has gained a strong reputation as an autonomous and technically competent regulator for energy and mining infrastructure over the last 20 years. The regulator has evolved by absorbing new functions and developing new competencies, mirroring a shift in national policies from a narrow focus on infrastructure expansion and investment attraction to wider goals of universal access and affordability.

This review considers that Osinergmin has absorbed its new functions with a relatively high degree of success. Following a period of growth in size and functions, it is only natural that Osinergmin should assess its strategic objectives and role as a step forward in its institutional maturity. The key challenge for Osinergmin is to progress its development from a reactive organisation, competently able to address emergencies and resolve crises, to a proactive institution with a clear vision for the energy and mining sectors and a relationship of trust with its key stakeholders.

In doing so, there are a number of issues requiring renewed attention and action. Osinergmin needs to ensure that it retains the full confidence of all actors in the energy and mining sectors, thereby providing the degree of stability necessary to ensure the participation of businesses, consumers and other stakeholders in these markets. This is particularly important at a time of high instability in the Peruvian public sector.

Internally, Osinergmin needs to strive for organisational frameworks, management systems and capabilities that allow the regulator to engage effectively with current and emerging challenges. Osinergmin and the government can promote initiatives that guarantee the regulator's autonomy while ensuring greater accountability, including through more transparent and robust external governance arrangements. In addition, enhanced and more formal co-ordination mechanisms with other sector regulators and market players are essential for limiting, and ultimately resolving, the conflicts that may arise.

Role and objectives

Osinergmin's mandate

Osinergmin is one of four regulators with autonomy from central government created in the 1990s to oversee Peru's transition to a liberalised economy. Osinergmin and the other economic regulators share a legal framework (*Ley marco de los organismos reguladores de la inversión privada en los servicios públicos*, Law 27332 or LMOR) that grants them technical, administrative, economic and financial autonomy but places them under the aegis of the Presidency of the Council of Ministers (PCM).

As the safety and economic regulator for energy and mining infrastructure Osinergmin's role, mandate and structure have changed substantially over the past 20 years:

- In 1997, Osinergmin was created to oversee infrastructure safety and compliance with environmental regulations and occupational health and safety in the energy sector.
- In 2000, soon after its creation, the regulator was given additional functions in tariff setting for the regulated energy markets.
- In 2004-05, Peru's energy landscape changed dramatically since natural gas reserves first came to fruition. Osinergmin began supervising the hydrocarbon sector in 1997. As of 2017, the sector produced 70% of all primary energy in the country and is the input to an increasing share of electricity generation.
- In 2006, further competencies were attributed to Osinergmin with the management of auctions for renewable energy; over time, national policies have placed emphasis on decentralised solar energy in rural areas.
- In 2007, the supervision of the mining sector (medium and large mines) was transferred to Osinergmin, in part due to the regulator's strong reputation as a technical body.
- In 2009 and 2011, because of institutional reforms and the creation of new public entities, the regulator forewent some regulatory functions that it originally had been granted, namely environmental and occupational health supervision.

Since 2012, the Ministry of Energy and Mining (MEM) granted Osinergmin the additional role of administering the Energy Social Inclusion Fund (FISE) and supervising its deployment. The main policy goal of FISE is to overcome Peru's energy gap between the country's rural and urban zones. Osinergmin created a team in charge of FISE that seems capable of managing the fund effectively. Their mandate, initially only temporary, has been extended every year. However, the regulator's role in the programme may raise doubts about its independence from central government as MEM directs Osinergmin in all aspects of the programme. Furthermore, by means of a Decree (*Decreto de Urgencia*) in 2017, after the concession contract failed, the Executive granted Osinergmin the additional function of nominating an assets administrator of the Southern Pipeline (*Gasoducto Sur Peruano*) concession.

Osinergmin's role has changed, incorporating new teams and functions, but an organisation-wide review has not been carried out – this can affect the regulator's role and purpose in the eyes of all stakeholders. Osinergmin has grown in size and mandate, adding departments and teams that were previously housed elsewhere. In addition, FISE activities tend to spill over to other departments within Osinergmin which are not, on paper, involved with the programme (for example, tariff regulation experts are called upon to advice on finance schemes for gas prices). Whilst the Board and executive team of Osinergmin have made some changes to internal functions and governance, there has not been, to date, a thorough and holistic review. Without this, there are risks associated with a mandate growing in a patchwork fashion, including that stakeholders (government, industry, citizens) may lose sight of the central purpose of the regulator, damaging role clarity.

Limitations and requirements imposed by government, coupled with growth in scope and functions, could hinder rapid and effective decision-making. Compounding the growth in scope, whilst the applicable legal framework (LMOR) ostensibly grants Osinergmin technical, administrative, economic and financial autonomy, it nonetheless requires the PCM's approval for a number of critical matters. These include limitations on budget expenditure and industry funding arrangements, internal organisational arrangements, and the design and administration of key processes. These requirements may hinder rapid and effective decision-making and provides for potential pinch points to challenge the independence of the regulator. Ultimately, these limitations could undermine confidence in the regulator and the efficacy of the markets that it regulates and the government's ability to deliver on its objectives.

Recommendations:

- ***Proactively engage*** with stakeholders to communicate more effectively Osinergmin's core mandate and functions in economic and safety regulation. Constructive engagement can improve stakeholders' understanding of the role played by the regulator, in an effort to preserve the regulator's legal and de facto autonomy.
- ***Undertake*** a holistic mapping review of Osinergmin's mandate to ensure that it has the appropriate resources, structures, systems and capabilities it requires to deliver on its growing role and objectives. For instance, the regulator could assess the impact of uncertainty surrounding its role as administrator of FISE, including the extent to which the renewal of Osinergmin's mandate on a temporary basis affects the regulator's resources, autonomy and perception by external stakeholders.

Institutional co-ordination

Osinergmin operates within a complex governance system that requires interactions with several public agencies and departments and within a policy framework that has been rapidly evolving. Osinergmin regularly liaises with the oversight body in the Executive (PCM) as well as the Ministry of Finance (MEF) on issues of budget and organisation; with MEM on policy and technical matters; with *Indecopi* on consumer protection and competition; and with *ProInversion* in relation to investment promotion, including concessions. Congress can also call upon Osinergmin through the two permanent committees that oversee its areas of competence. Interaction with other institutions is informal often depends on personal relationships and, on occasion, the establishment of ad-hoc working groups, such as the one formed in 2017 by MEM, Osinergmin and the Economic Operating Committee of the National Interconnected System (*Comité de Operación Económica del Sistema Interconectado Nacional, COES*)[1] to review and propose updates to the Law on Electric Concessions.

In light of the reallocation of roles among supervisory authorities, the need for institutional co-ordination has become even more pressing. The government has transferred environmental and occupational health competencies from Osinergmin to the Agency for Environmental Assessment and Control (*Organismo de Evaluación y Fiscalización Ambiental, OEFA*) and the National Superintendence of Labour Inspection (*Superintendencia Nacional de Fiscalización Laboral, SUNAFIL*) respectively. This has limited the scope of Osinergmin's regulatory and supervisory powers and increased the number of public agencies with whom regulated companies and users interact.

Recommendations:

- ***Set up*** a forum of economic regulators of Peru to harmonise external communication on the role of economic regulators, share good practices (e.g. in regulatory management tools), and jointly advocate for governance-related topics as relevant. The leadership of the group could rotate between the regulatory authorities and the group should aim to focus on concrete deliverable and activities, rather than setting up a bureaucratic system of collaboration.
- ***Develop*** specific instruments to ensure more structured and regular co-ordination among the public agencies (OEFA, SUNAFIL) involved in the supervision of the energy and mining sectors, as well as the COES in the electricity sector. These instruments can include the following:
  - Regular working groups both at high level (e.g. presidents, executive leadership) and at a technical level (e.g. area managers, experts), providing a recognised channel for inter-agency communication and a commonly agreed timeline to co-ordinate strategies and actions;
  - Memoranda of Understanding between Osinergmin and other entities, establishing more formal co-ordination mechanisms on common issues such as sharing information and good practices on supervision schedules, data requests and emergency responses, avoiding ah-hoc agreements whenever joint action is required.

Box 1. Examples of co-ordination among regulatory agencies

The challenges faced by regulators often transcend sectoral and geographical boundaries; hence, greater co-ordination and collaboration are needed. There are a number of experiences with co-ordination among regulatory agencies domestically, including:

- **Australia:** the Utility Regulators Forum aims to facilitate the exchange of information, understanding of the issues faced by regulators, consistency in the application of regulatory functions and the review of new ideas about regulatory practices. The newsletter of the forum is published quarterly and contains articles on common challenges, summaries of recent journal articles on regulatory matters, and updates on regulatory decisions.

- **France**: the *Club des Régulateurs* provides a forum for both established and new economic regulators to share common problems with a few thematic meetings every year, most recently on issues of data privacy and data handling. A third party, currently an academic institution, hosts it.
- **Mexico**: following the OECD's peer review of three energy regulators (ASEA, CNH and CRE), a permanent co-ordination group for the energy sector was established, leading to joint briefs, inspections and an exchange programme, better equipping regulators to implement wide-ranging sector reforms.
- **United Kingdom (Scotland)**: As part of the Strategic Review of charges for 2021-2027, stakeholders in Scotland meet on a monthly basis to ensure collective buy-in and collaborative working around the key issues faced by the water and wastewater sectors. The meetings involve high-level representatives from the water operator (Scottish Water), economic regulator (The Water Industry Commission for Scotland, WICS), the quality regulator (Drinking Water Quality Regulator for Scotland, DWQR) and the environment regulator (Scottish Environment Protection Agency, SEPA), as well as the Customer Forum and the consumers association. More granular analysis from the working groups feeds into those high-level discussions.
- **Ireland**: a new Economic Regulators' Network is convened around four times a year and hosts discussions on common challenges such as the legal interpretation of new regulations. Participants recognise that further work is needed to address technical regulatory issues across sectors.

Source: Network of Economic Regulators (NER) at the OECD.

Box 2. Co-ordination in the Mexican energy sector

The recent energy reform that opened the oil and gas sector to private investment in Mexico in 2013 enhanced the institutional set-up of the existing economic regulators: the upstream regulator, the National Commission for Hydrocarbons (*Comisión Nacional de Hidrocarburos*, CNH) and the downstream regulator, the Energy Regulation Commission (*Comisión Reguladora de Energía*, CRE). The reform also created a new cross-cutting technical regulator to oversee safety and environmental protection throughout the whole hydrocarbon value chain: the Safety, Energy and Environment Agency (*Agencia de Seguridad, Energía y Ambiente*, ASEA).

Recently the three regulators have come together and formalised a Cooperation Agreement and a joint working group (the Group) around four main objectives:

1. Planning: to share a common vision of the future and plan accordingly.
2. Operational co-ordination: to address operating priorities in a timely manner.
3. Resources: to address common necessities concerning talent attraction and retention and financial autonomy.
4. Conflict resolution: to address and resolve conflicts between regulators.

The Group is chaired by a rotating presidency, whose leadership changes every six months.

One of the common tools now available to the energy sector in Mexico – and the result of inter-agency co-ordination – is a "one-stop-shop" electronic portal where companies can register and fulfill all administrative and reporting obligations. The website connects users to specific regulatory agencies where filings must be made. This tool facilitates the interaction of industry participants and regulatory agencies. Each agency conserves and executes its regulatory role, and companies are granted faster access to all agencies, with the confidence of being directed to the appropriate regulatory authority depending on the subject matter. The Group has also proven to be a good mechanism for putting together a package of statutory and legal proposals that aim at bolstering the integrated system of regulators institutional set-up and independence. These proposals are being jointly discussed with relevant government stakeholders.

Source: Information provided by the Mexican National Commission for Hydrocarbons, (OECD, 2018[1]).

Strategic objectives

Osinergmin sets out its medium to long-term strategic objectives in the Strategic Institutional Plan (*Plan Estratégico Institucional,* PEI) which acts as the main reference framework for the management of its internal activities (see Table 1) Osinergmin's current PEI runs from 2014 to 2021. The regulator prepared the PEI at a time of changing priorities for energy policy nationally, given the increasing importance of universal access and affordability concerns alongside investment attraction and system efficiency laid out in the National Energy Plan 2014-25 and the National Energy Policy 2010-40. As such, the PEI rightly aims to align the long-term strategies and goals of the regulator with those of the government and sets out initiatives to achieve those goals.

Table 1. Osinergmin's Strategic Plan

Category of focus	Strategic objective
Stakeholders	1. Achieve credibility and trust of the society in the role of Osinergmin. 2. Develop rules and processes, with autonomy, transparency and predictability for the business sector. 3. Promote the improvement of coverage at the national level of sufficient, affordable and quality services. 4. Serve the requirements of stakeholders in an understandable, quick and efficient form. 5. Encourage that the operations of the companies are safe for the community, workers and the environment.
Internal processes	6. Integrate and improve the regulation, supervision and audit processes. 7. Incorporate a long-term global vision in energy and mining that promotes the development of initiatives for a sustainable industry policy. 8. Promote decentralisation and linkage processes between consumers and companies. 9. Strengthen communications with stakeholders. 10. Develop the conditions for regional energy interconnection. 11. Monitoring and regulating investment commitments in new infrastructure.
Human resources development, learning and technology	12. Develop innovation and creativity through organisational learning and knowledge management. 13. Build an attractive organisation through the professional and personal development of its employees. 14. Have adequate information systems and technologies that provide support to Osinergmin's activities.
Financial resources	15. Use the budget efficiently.

Source: Information provided by Osinergmin, 2018.

The values of commitment, excellence, service, integrity and autonomy underpin the strategy. The PEI has a balance of input-related, process-related and output-related objectives. Five objectives are devoted to improving stakeholder relationship (through greater trust, autonomy and transparency) and an additional internal process indicator focuses on better communication with stakeholders, hence placing emphasis on the outward-facing aspects of the regulator's activity.

Osinergmin has an active communications strategy to convey information about its work and increase the reputation of the regulator, while also providing simple and easy ways to report problems by users with services. Osinergmin is very active on social media with over 45 000 followers on Twitter, 24 000 on LinkedIn, and 62 500 followers on Facebook. The regulator has also launched both app-based (*Facilito Electricidad*) and SMS-based (*Tikuy Rikuy*) services enabling users to report issues to the electricity company that provides the service – subsequently, the information reaches Osinergmin as the regulator supervises compliance. The regulator also provides information to the wider public on matters that it does not directly regulate, such as petrol pump prices allowing drivers to find the cheapest in their area (*Facilito Combustible*). Their communication in inclusive, utilising methods to communicate with disabled persons as well as non-Spanish speaking communities, such as the Quechuan population.

Recommendations:

- ***Carry out*** a mid-term evaluation of the PEI in order to:
  - ***Prioritise*** objectives more systematically across the short, medium and long-term, thereby providing a timeline for actions linked to each objective;
  - ***Develop*** in more detail a forward-looking vision for the sector, reasserting the regulator's role to provide a predictable framework for investors and citizens within the policy directions set by government – and link strategic objectives to such vision;
  - ***More closely link*** budgeting and planning to forecast needs and minimise risks.

Input

Financial resources

Osinergmin is funded by contributions from the industry, set at a rate approved by the PCM upon proposal of the regulator. The Law caps contributions to 1% of total industry turnover but Osinergmin has, since 2013, proposed specific rates for different sectors well below maximum thresholds based on an estimation of its funding needs. In 2016, the regulator also proposed marginally declining rates across all sectors for 2017-19 (see Table 2), responding in part to industry's concerns that rates were too high. Revenues from contributions constitute around 90% of Osinergmin's total budget and the regulator does not receive any funding from government.

Table 2. Rate of regulatory contributions to Osinergmin, 2017-19

Sector	Rate of regulatory contribution (% of annual income)		
	2017	2018	2019
Electricity	0.52%	0.51%	0.50%
Hydrocarbons			
• Import and production of fuels, including liquefied petroleum gas (LPG) and natural gas (LNG)	0.36%	0.35%	0.34%
• Concessionaires of hydrocarbons transport and distribution via pipelines	0.57%	0.56%	0.55%
Mining	0.15%	0.14%	0.13%

Source: Information provided by Osinergmin, 2018.

Osinergmin plans its budget on a three-year rolling basis, balancing the needs of each department (bottom-up) and revenue projections (top-down) from the proposed industry contributions. As such, industry contributions are not determined nor adjusted in accordance with an *ex post* cost recovery principle and, in any given year, resources may exceed or fail to meet actual needs. However, Osinergmin's management agrees that the regulator has had sufficient funds to cover costs and meet its objectives historically.

The main indicator that the Executive monitors is budget execution, but at the same time, central government rules raise some concerns with respect to the regulator's ability to use its budget fully. Budget execution at Osinergmin was around 90% in 2015 and 2016 but below 80% in 2017 (see Table 3). However, existing public sector-wide rules, such as on salary scales, as well as recent austerity measures (that may or may not be temporary in nature), affect Osinergmin's ability to execute its budget. These include:

- Limitations to the budget for communications and outreach, resulting in fewer public awareness events and the decision, *inter alia*, not to produce an executive summary and print out hard copies of the annual report
- Limitations to the budget for travel expenses, limiting the ability of Osinergmin's senior staff to participate in international fora and networks

Table 3. Osinergmin Annual Budget and Execution, 2015-17

Year	2015	2016	2017
Budget (million PEN)	328.5	349.5	402.6
Execution (%)	90.9%	89.5%	77.7%

Source: Information provided by Osinergmin, 2018.

Additionally since 2017, the *Ley de Equilibrio Financiero* requires that all surplus funds of public institutions (including those collected from industry) be returned to the Treasury if not executed in a given fiscal year. Government needs to renew this measure explicitly every year. When coupled with austerity measures this can translates into Osinergmin accumulating a surplus at the end of the year and having to forward any unspent funds to the Treasury. In 2017, Government also directed Osinergmin to return its accumulated surplus from previous years.

Recommendations:

- ***Take*** a proactive stance in order to explain the impacts of emerging uncertainty in public financing and fiscal rules on budget execution. The regulator should seek clarity on the extent and duration of recently imposed measures, document to Government the direct impacts of those measures on its activities and advocate that the principles of cost-recovery and transparency should be key drivers of its funding model.
- ***Co-ordination*** among regulators in Peru on this issue would be beneficial. For example, regulators could advocate that the resources collected by regulators and coming from industry contributions should only be directed towards programmes in the same industry. There are numerous examples of industry levy models from OECD countries that Peruvian regulators can look at. The risk is that, otherwise, industry will perceive its contributions as a de facto tax.
- ***Map*** Osinergmin's costs against predicted resources and, where shortfalls are predicted, evaluate future needs. In light of funding uncertainty, prioritisation as part of the annual plans becomes ever more important. Prioritisation can be based on more specific "value for money" assessments of different expenditure items and detailed costing of regulatory and supervisory activities. Measures of funding gaps and value for money can accompany budget execution statistics as a measure of success.

Box 3. Budgeting in Portugal and Canada

The Portuguese Water and Waste Services Regulation Authority (ERSAR)

In 2013, the approval of a new legislative framework for public services sector regulators (Law No. 67/2013) has brought new dispositions on the independence of regulators in Portugal. The law established that these authorities would have administrative, financial, management autonomy, and organic, functional and technical independence to perform their role. The law specifically establishes that these authorities should have their own boards, staff and property, as well as regulatory, inspection and sanctioning powers.

Regarding financial independence, this law establishes that regulators' funding should come from levies in the sectors where they act. Therefore, Portuguese regulators are funded by the regulated market through levies charged by the regulator according to the dimension of each operator. For instance, ERSAR, the Water and Waste Services Regulation Authority, is funded through levies that are charged to water and waste services operators according to the population served and to the activity level of each operator. This practice brings additional independence, since the regulator's activity is perceived as a service to the regulated sectors. The regulator considers these levies an admissible cost for tariff determination, which means that, ultimately, they are transferred to consumers in the tariff they pay. These levies represent less than 1% of the monthly charges paid by consumers, which is considered a very reasonable value for money for the regulation "service".

According to ERSAR's statutes (Law No. 10/2014), if there is a net surplus from the annual budget execution, these amounts should be transferred for the following year and should be used in the development of specific actions aiming to benefit the sector, namely technical capacitation of the operators and other stakeholders. The net surplus could also be returned to the consumers in the form of lower prices.

National Energy Board of Canada (NEB)

Pursuant to the regulatory scheme in place, the Canadian NEB's cost recovery mechanism is premised on commodity charging costs that are allocated to specific entities within those sectors (oil – oil pipelines, gas – gas pipelines, etc.). Companies pay their share of recoverable costs to the Consolidated Revenue Fund of Canada, through greenfield levies, fixed levies (small, intermediate companies and other commodities) or proportional levies (large companies). The allocation of costs to commodity categories is based on time spent on each commodity.

The NEB also has an advisory committee, which is composed of the staff from the regulator and representatives of the regulated companies, that reviews planned expenditures and discusses cost recovery issues. The NEB does not receive this funding directly from companies; rather, it receives its appropriations through Parliament, on an annual basis.

Source: Information provided by ERSAR, (OECD, 2018[11]), *Driving Performance at Ireland's Comission for Regulation and Utilities*, OECD Publishing, Paris, https://doi.org/10.1787/9789264190061-en.

Human resources

Osinergmin's employees have recorded a low level of turnover and a high level of satisfaction in recent years, testimony to the regulator's efforts to provide an attractive and rewarding working environment. Osinergmin is able to attract competent analysts and support staff at the entry and middle levels. Osinergmin offers its employees a generous benefits package that includes full health care coverage for employees and their families (subject to co-payments), training programmes supported by corporate partnerships with universities, and team building initiatives (for employees hired until Law 728, as discussed below). In addition, growth opportunities are present thanks to frequent openings across departments. For 16 years, Osinergmin has also operated a national recruitment programme for engineering, economics and law graduates through internship programmes often leading to full employment. Osinergmin has a robust performance assessment system that links staff objectives to the PEI. Thanks to all these efforts, Osinergmin's staff turnover rate has been stable (around 16% for all staff and 4% for permanent staff over 2015-17) and staff satisfaction reached a 10-year high in 2017.

The recruitment of senior staff poses more challenges, mainly because salaries have been frozen in nominal terms by the government since 2006 and a dual employment system exists. Osinergmin employs around 680 professional staff members (more than 100 new positions were added over 2015-18). Staff are mostly hired through open and transparent procedures based on a recruitment skills model, whereby the recruitment committee indicates the selected candidate for the General Manager to formally appoint. The President directly appoints some senior management positions (*puestos de confianza*). Appointees need to have certain qualifications and skills that the internal operating manual describes in detail. Osinergmin has two vastly different employment regimes for contracts: staff members hired under Law 728 have permanent contracts and benefits as described above, in line with private sector conditions. Meanwhile staff hired under Law 1057 are only granted renewable 6-month contracts and lower benefits. The existence of parallel frameworks may be problematic for accountability (hiring) and incentives for staff (remuneration, benefits). Law 30057 (*Ley del Servicio Civil*) was approved in 2013 with the aim of establishing a single labour regime for civil servants including staff of economic regulators. Implementation, led by the public agency SERVIR, has been slow.

Recommendations:

- ***Continue*** to attract and retain competent staff, regularly updating existing plans for maintaining technical expertise, monitoring salaries compared to the private sector, addressing current needs and future expectations in collaboration with existing staff. Planning for technical expertise is particularly important as the regulator competes with the private sector for specialised and technical staff in the energy and mining sectors, where salaries can be significantly higher than national averages
- ***Continue*** investing in recruitment strategies in order to remain an attractive choice for new graduates. Graduate programmes, including through specific agreements with universities across Peru, are useful to ensure that new skills and new thinking can enter the institution as well as to diversify the workforce.

Process

Decision making

By design, the members of the Board are appointed on staggered contracts following a balanced process involving different state actors. Board members are selected by a multi-step process with checks and balances that includes review by an inter-institutional selection committee, submission of selected candidates to the President of the Republic by the President of the Council of Ministers, appointment by the President of the Republic by Supreme Decree, and finally endorsement by the PCM, MEF and MEM. The Osinergmin Board normally comprises six members (one of whom is the President). At the time of writing, one position is vacant and the other five members have the following background: two lawyers, two engineers, and one economist. There have been no women on the Board in the last ten years.

Board meetings are not very frequent and are dominated by operational matters, with little time dedicated to strategic planning and longer-term thinking. Board members receive remuneration to meet twice per month, significantly limiting their capacity to weigh in on complex strategic and technical decisions. Requests can be made to meet additionally under extraordinary circumstances by the President or a majority of its members; although this happens, the law forbids any additional remuneration for this time. The President is the only member of the Board who is remunerated on a full-time basis and can have a number of advisors. The other four members have no supporting staff for their duties as members of the Osinergmin Board and their internal requests for information to different departments can at times take a long time before they are processed.

Recommendations:

- ***Assess*** whether the activity and duties of the Board reflect its mandate and structure. In its current configuration, the Board appears to have a hybrid model with elements of both executive and non-executive arrangements. Building on the professional experience of Board members, the by-monthly meetings should focus more on strategic discussions to advance and improve Osinergmin's actions and less on detailed operational decisions. The Board could look for opportunities to delegate some of those decisions (particularly the more operational and non-controversial ones where a precedent already exists).

- ***Make*** existing advisory resources available to Board members, as already provided by the internal manual (MOF). Board members should be able to access succinct and consolidated information ahead of meetings to support more informed decision-making. Advisory resources could also help Board members dedicate more of their limited time to strategic matters.

Internal organisation and management

Osinergmin is directly managed by the President of the Board, with the support of the General Manager (GM). The President appoints the GM and other senior management of the organisation without open recruitment (and can remove them from their posts), approves the institutional budget, balance sheets and financial statements as well as the Institutional Management Plan and administrative policies. The President and the GM chair a weekly meeting with Osinergmin senior management. The GM is responsible for the legal, administrative, communication and technology departments of Osinergmin and plans, organises, manages, executes and supervises the administrative, operational, economic and financial activities of Osinergmin. He or she prepares draft annual reports, budgets and senior management recruitment decisions for decision by the President. The GM also oversees the work of the economic and legal analysis departments. Therefore, a large number of decision-making functions are concentrated in these two executive positions, placing very high expectations on the individuals and over-centralising risk for the organisation.

Osinergmin has demonstrated institutional agility and adaptability through changes in mandate and functions that have required organisational change. The regulator has integrated new teams and competencies in recent years. It has done so by striving to develop common guidelines, ways of working and co-ordination processes. The sense of pride that brings together Osinergmin's employees is an important asset to achieve this goal. However, as recognised in the PEI, more needs to be done to foster a shared institutional culture. Some of the concrete steps currently underway to achieve this goal include:

- The application of similar legal requirements, quality management processes and analytical tools across all departments;
- The introduction of regulatory management tools common to all rule-making and tariff-setting processes, most notably a common Regulatory Impact Assessment (RIA) methodology;
- The creation of a joint Energy and Mining Observatory (OEM) pulling together all the data collected by the regulator and fully accessible by both citizens and businesses;
- Streamlined communications and outreach campaigns through the official channels (TV, radio, online) and increasingly through apps and social media, as well as greater accessibility by making available guides in Braille.

Effective communication of objectives and strategies is essential. This review calls for a more robust external relations strategy that communicates the core objectives of the regulator, greater co-ordination with other institutions and a renewed focus on stakeholder engagement as well as regular liaison with the regulated sectors. This will not be possible unless the regulator invests further human and financial resources in external liaison and institutional relations functions. Currently different departments within

Osinergmin interact with different external actors and the Communications and Inter-Institutional Relations Department comprises only nine employees.

The Regional Offices under the Energy Supervision Department have promoted Osinergmin's presence in the regions but their role is at times unclear. The fact that over 20% of the organisation's budget goes to Regional Offices and that their staff numbers are growing reflects widespread recognition that they have the potential to contribute to improving citizens' awareness of Osinergmin. Regional Offices have indeed been providing decentralised support to the most remote areas, including in case of emergencies and user complaints. They have also managed the creation of the Energy and Mining Observatory (OEM). However, some of their competences are not clearly defined and overlap with other departments. For instance, it is unclear which issues should be resolved at the local level or in Lima in the case of user complaints.

Another area for improvement is on the management of the Users Council (*Consejo de Usuarios,* established by Law for all independent regulators). Osinergmin complies with the legal requirement to have at least one Users Council, and its only Council comprises five members from a number of civil society organisations, industrial associations, and professional body associations. However, the Council does not provide meaningful inputs to the regulator's decision-making processes. The potentially positive impact of the Council is not being fully exploited. Advisory bodies and councils of users exist around OECD countries as an effective means for the regulator to keep their finger on the pulse of the market and inform policy development. This is especially important in the energy and mining sectors where environmental and social impacts can deeply affect indigenous and rural populations, who then react with protests and blocking new developments.

Recommendations:

- ***Map*** roles, obligations and functions of the executive management team (President, General Manager, Board Members, and Department Managers) to the various areas of responsibility of the organisation with a view to spread executive responsibilities more widely and broaden the existing decision-making structure.
- ***Set up*** appropriate accountability measures, aiming to establish formal mechanisms for quality control of internal decisions. These should be formalised in a Board/Management Charter, starting from the existing *Manual de Organización y Funciones* (MOF). Ongoing work towards the adoption of international standards and the promotion of an integrated management system goes in the right direction by streamlining the regulator's processes and ways of working.
- ***Strengthen and clarify*** some of Osinergmin's internal functions. In particular, the regulator would benefit from:
  - ***Strengthening*** the role of inter-institutional relations by leading the co-ordination with other supervisory authorities and liaising more closely with government and Congress. The existing Communications and Inter-Institutional relations Department could take up this role but would require strong support and leadership from senior management as well as an assessment of the need for additional resources.

  - ***Clarifying*** the competencies of the Regional Offices vis-à-vis other Departments, making their work more crosscutting as part of Osinergmin's efforts to improve its public recognition, and assessing the impact of their advocacy activities on litigation and user complaints.
- ***Reform*** the Users Council to advance Osinergmin's practices of consultation and engagement by attracting new applicants and redefining roles for the 2020-22 Users Council would advance. For example, the Council could be assigned well-defined tasks linked to specific regulatory interventions and aimed at eliciting views and evidence from users and consumers. Participation could be broadened to research institutes and think tanks. One of the areas of interest could be involving users in expressing their views about local infrastructure projects before conflicts arise. Osinergmin should assign clear responsibilities for managing the Council(s), and match this with resources (e.g. funding, training).

Regulatory quality processes

Osinergmin has been a pioneer amongst government agencies in Peru at implementing regulatory impact assessments (RIA), along with other regulatory agencies and the PCM. In response to the 2016 *OECD Regulatory Review of Peru*, the PCM began developing a Regulatory Quality Assessment (RQA) framework that implements measures for simplifying administrative processes, including a requirement for assessing the impacts as well as conduct stock reviews and *ex post* evaluations of regulations that add administrative processes. Osinergmin, independently and in parallel developed a manual with guidelines for applying Regulatory Impact Assessments (RIA) to all regulatory decisions and not just administrative processes. In 2016, the manual and guidelines were released, which allow for multiple types of analysis ranging from a full cost-benefit analysis to a 'mini-RIA,' whereby the decision is proportional to the issue at hand. As of October 2018, one full RIA was completed, a second full RIA was underway, 16 mini-RIAs were completed and a further 18 were underway.

Osinergmin practices stakeholder engagement consistently at the later stages of rule making, but there is no permanent forum with regulated entities to discuss early regulatory developments. All regulators are required to publish new norms and regulations in the Official Gazette and on the institutional website 30 days before their entry into force. Where applicable, a RIA is included in the supporting documentation. Osinergmin opens the consultation period for comments and logs all comments received and actions taken in response in a 'comments matrix', which is published alongside the final regulation for transparency. Osinergmin does not usually conduct early-stage consultations and mainly relies on an open-door policy to encourage regulated entities to provide feedback on the sector or regulatory developments, which places the onus on the entities to be proactive about providing this feedback. However, in the case of tariff-setting decisions, Osinergmin's engagement process includes early proposals from the regulated companies, the pre-publication of resolutions and supporting documentation for comments.

The PCM RQA only requires *ex post* evaluations for administrative procedures in Peru, while Osinergmin has conducted evaluations voluntarily on some of its regulatory decisions and funds it administers. In accordance with the RQA, regulations adding administrative procedures must be reviewed every three years, with some exceptions. In Osinergmin, the Department for Economic and Policy Analysis (GPAE) produces *Policy Evaluation Documents (DEPs)*, which are evaluations conducted on a case-by-case basis. DEPs seek to quantify *ex post* the impacts of supervisions and control activities to assess their effectiveness at meeting intended goals. Additionally, both investment programmes FISE and FOSE (Electric Social Compensation Fund) must undergo impact analyses in accordance with methodologies defined by MEF. The PCM RQA also requires government agencies to undergo a review of their stock of regulations and, at the time of writing, Osinergmin is working with the PCM to advance this review.

Recommendations:

- ***Continue*** to invest in improving Osinergmin's regulatory management tools and processes. This will provide returns in terms of transparency, accountability and engagement. The GPAE co-ordinates Osinergmin's efforts in developing the practice of RIA and ex post evaluation. It is important for the Department to strengthen this role with appropriate powers and responsibilities, and push for full implementation of the recent guidelines across all regulatory areas.
- ***Outline*** a process for regular external engagement and dialogue with stakeholders, particularly outside the tariff-setting processes and at the early stages of rule making. Extensive consultation before implementing any new rules is useful to minimise future areas of misunderstanding of the norms and therefore litigation. Structured dialogue around planned infrastructure projects can also help Osinergmin understand and tackle the root causes of those investment projects currently blocked due to force majeure.

Box 4. Consumer engagement in economic regulatory determinations in electricity regulation in Australia

The Australian Energy Regulator (AER) has always enabled consumers to make submissions to its consultations, such as at public forums, draft determinations on regulatory proposals and issues papers. However, as part of the Better Regulation program in 2013, the AER introduced a series of measures to strengthen consumer engagement in the energy sector. This included internally focussed measures, such as establishing a Consumer Challenge Panel (CCP) and Consumer Reference Groups, as well as providing clear guidance for regulated businesses on consumer engagement through the production of a Consumer Engagement Guideline.

The CCP was the main institution established to advise the AER on consumer interests in regulatory processes. The CCP is a panel of experts appointed to champion the long-term interests of consumers, rather than an advocacy body for consumers. The CCP's main role is to analyse whether regulatory proposals are aligned with the long-term interests of consumers, as well as examine the effectiveness of related consumer engagement activities. While it is not a decision making body, the CCP advises the AER on the interests and concerns of consumers in relation to broader issues. For example, a subpanel of three members was formed to advice on the development of cost reflective pricing for electricity distribution networks.

In addition to the CCP, the AER also established Consumer Reference Groups to provide guidance on specific issues. For example, in 2017 the AER established a Consumer Reference Group to provide input to the review of the rate of return guideline. This group directly engaged with industry bodies and was given resources to commission consultancy support to establish an aligned position on behalf of all customers. The group was able to establish evidence to influence elements of this review, such as the averaging period for the risk free rate, for the long run interests of all consumers.

The Consumer Engagement Guideline outlines key principles and components to inform regulated business' strategies and processes. The guideline acknowledges that the appropriate level of consumer engagement in any situation depends on factors like the objectives, timeframes, resources, and level of interest. So it encourages business to consider its objective and capacity for engaging with consumers (including the number of consumers) when contemplating different approaches. In addition to exploring the appropriate level of engagement, the Consumer Engagement Guideline contains four best practice principles to guide engagement strategies. These principles are that the engagement should be clear, accurate and timely communication; accessible and inclusive; transparent; and, measurable.

Source: Information provided by the Australian Energy Regulator (AER).

Inspections, enforcement and compliance

Enforcement and inspections on the safety of energy and mining infrastructure are core functions of Osinergmin, but the regulator often delivers this function in a vacuum. There is little co-ordination between different inspection authorities (Osinergmin, OEFA and SUNAFIL) on planning joint schedules and data requests. This can place burdens on regulated entities that face overlapping data requests and re-inspections on the same issues. The lack of co-ordination can also translate in poor use of public resources.

In addition, the proliferation of binding standards and new norms can reduce the regulator's ability to manage the volume and frequency of inspections and can undermine its ability to enforce standards and norms effectively. A growing number of requirements also results in reduced predictability for industry players. Altogether, Osinergmin may find itself struggling to ensure compliance and relying heavily on the threat of sanctions in its relationship with supervised entities. The regulator recognises this risk and aims to revise its approach by strengthening the role of preventative actions.

Recommendations:

- ***Improve*** the efficiency of enforcement and inspections by minimising burden on regulated entities and maximising effectiveness of public resources. Co-operation with OEFA and SUNAFIL (as described in previous recommendations) can result in better information sharing, with agencies acting as "eyes and ears" for others. Mapping the enforcement and inspection journey from a user/regulate perspective could help identify opportunities for joint interventions that maximise impacts while minimising burden.
- ***Develop*** an Enforcement and Compliance Strategy and communicate this to all stakeholders through a Statement of Approach, updated annually to reflect the strategic priorities of the organisation (e.g. which aspects of safety may be the focus of this year's reviews). This will establish transparent working arrangements ahead of physical inspections, working towards the goal of establishing a closer working relationship with regulated entities as detailed in the PEI.

- ***Make*** accidents, disasters and emergencies prevention a key priority through soft instruments such as the establishment of a safety culture and technical recommendations (non-binding instruments) on processes and procedures, in order to change behaviours over time in the regulated entities. The 2018 OECD Regulatory Enforcement and Inspections Toolkit provides a useful checklist (see Box 6).

Box 5. The ACCC's compliance and enforcement strategy

In Australia, the ACCC (Australian Competition & Consumer Commission) developed a compliance and enforcement strategy that is communicated to all stakeholders. The agency uses four integrated strategies to achieve the compliance objectives:

- Encouraging compliance with the law by educating and informing consumers and businesses about their rights and responsibilities.
- Enforcing the law, including resolution of possible contraventions both administratively and by litigation and other formal enforcement outcomes.
- Undertaking market studies or reporting on emerging competition or consumer issues with a view to identifying any market failures and how to address them, and to support and inform the compliance and enforcement measures and identify possible areas for policy consideration.
- Working with other agencies to implement these strategies, including through co-ordinated approaches.

The ACCC is selective in the matters to investigate and the sectors in which the agency engages in education and market analysis. The ACCC uses annual compliance and enforcement priorities to inform decision making in this regard.

In deciding which compliance or enforcement tool (or the combination of such tools) to use, the first priority is always to achieve the best possible outcome for the community and to manage risk proportionately. The ACCC's enforcement actions seek to maximise impact across an industry sector. For example, the agency uses the outcome of one court proceeding to encourage other industry participants in the sector to improve their practices.

The ACCC's role is to focus on those circumstances that will, or have the potential to, harm the competitive process or result in widespread consumer detriment. ACCC therefore exercises discretion to direct resources to matters that provide the greatest overall benefit.

Each year the ACCC reviews the compliance and enforcement priorities. Priorities are determined following external consultation and an assessment of existing or emerging issues and their impact on the regulated matters.

Source: (ACCC, 2018[21]), "Compliance & enforcement policy & priorities", https://www.accc.gov.au/about-us/australian-competition-consumer-commission/compliance-enforcement-policy-priorities#the-accc-s-compliance-and-enforcement-strategy.

Box 6. The 2018 OECD Regulatory Enforcement and Inspections Toolkit

The OECD Regulatory Enforcement and Inspections Toolkit offers government officials, regulators, stakeholders and experts a simple tool for assessing the level of development of the inspection and enforcement system in a given jurisdiction, institution or structure. It presents a checklist of 12 criteria to identify strengths and weaknesses as well as areas for improvement:

1. **Evidence-based enforcement:** Regulatory enforcement and inspections should be evidence-based and measurement-based: deciding what to inspect and how should be grounded in data and evidence, and results should be evaluated regularly.
2. **Selectivity:** Promoting compliance and enforcing rules should be left to market forces, private sector actions and civil society activities wherever possible: inspections and enforcement cannot take place everywhere and address everything, and there are many other ways to achieve regulations' objectives.
3. **Risk focus and proportionality**: Enforcement needs to be risk-based and proportionate: the frequency of inspections and the resources employed should be proportional to the level of risk, and enforcement actions should aim at reducing the actual risk posed by infractions.
4. **Responsive regulation**: Enforcement should be based on "responsive regulation" principles; that is, inspection enforcement actions should be modulated depending on the profile and behaviour of specific businesses.
5. **Long-term vision**: Governments should adopt policies on regulatory enforcement and inspections, and establish institutional mechanisms with clear objectives and a long-term strategy.
6. **Co-ordination and consolidation**: Inspection functions should be co-ordinated and, where needed, consolidated: less duplication and fewer overlaps will ensure a better use of public resources, minimise the burden on regulated subjects, and maximise effectiveness.
7. **Transparent governance**: Governance structures and human resources policies for regulatory enforcement should support transparency, professionalism, and results-oriented management. The execution of regulatory enforcement should be independent from political influence, and compliance promotion efforts should be rewarded.
8. **Information integration**: Information and communication technologies should be used to maximise a focus on risks, promote co-ordination and information sharing and ensure an optimal use of resources.
9. **Clear and fair process**: Governments should ensure that rules and processes for enforcement and inspections are clear. Coherent legislation to organise inspections and enforcement needs to be adopted and published, and the rights and obligations of officials and of businesses, clearly articulated.
10. **Compliance promotion**: Transparency and compliance should be promoted through the use of appropriate instruments such as guidance, toolkits and checklists.

11. **Professionalism**: Inspectors should be trained and managed to ensure professionalism, integrity, consistency and transparency. This requires substantial training focusing not only on technical but also on generic inspection skills, and official guidelines for inspectors to help ensure consistency and fairness.
12. **Reality check**: Institutions in charge of inspection and enforcement, and the regulatory enforcement and inspection system as a whole, should deliver the levels of performance expected from them – in terms of stakeholder satisfaction, efficiency (benefits/costs), and overall effectiveness (safety, health, environmental protection etc.).

Source: (OECD, 2018[3]), *OECD Regulatory Enforcement and Inspections Toolkit*, http://dx.doi.org/10.1787/9789264303959-en.

Appeals

Citizens and businesses have access to a dispute resolution system at a reasonable cost to adjudicate user and inter-company complaints as well as sanctions, while the Board handles appeals to tariffs imposed by the regulator. The different appellate bodies housed within Osinergmin are staffed with lawyers and engineers to hear and rule on matters presented to them.

A significant rise in the number of appeals is raising the toll of unresolved cases in all tribunals, including the JARU (1 522 unresolved cases in 2016 and 2 339 in 2017) and the TASTEM (407 unresolved cases in 2016 and 274 in 2017). Osinergmin has been addressing this issue by hiring extra resources in 2018, leading to a 20% increase in personnel working across tribunals. Osinergmin is also considering the reason behind the growth in litigation. The following four areas have been identified, and deserve further analysis leading to remedial action by the responsible departments:

- Complexity of the regulatory framework and a large number of new rules and norms issued each year leading to non-compliance
- A punitive supervision approach leading to a growing number of fines levied
- Delays in nominating some of the TSC (*Tribunal de Solución de Controversias)* members by the PCM
- The increase in activities in more remote areas raising awareness about consumer rights and ways to complain

Judicial review is the only recourse for citizens and companies dissatisfied with outcomes from the internal appeals process, which users and industry may also use to delay regulatory decisions. After the appellate bodies, businesses and citizens can further appeal through judicial reviews in administrative courts. Judicial reviews can scrutinise Osinergmin's and other regulators' decisions both on legality and merit grounds. As well, all sanctions can be appealed. This has led to some disagreements between Osinergmin and the courts in recent years, mainly in relation to the interpretation of norms in the electricity sector. In addition, the payment of user fees is suspended and no interest accrues on bills during a litigation process, providing an unintended incentive to seek and prolong judicial review.

Recommendation:

- ***Complete*** the ongoing investigation into the underlying reasons for an increase in disputes and take remedial action to address root causes. For instance, simplification of the regulatory framework and language could be a strategic goal for the coming years, as businesses have raised the issue of normative interpretation on several occasions. Improving information provision and dialogue with market players at the earlier stages of rule-making can also lead to better awareness on the part of citizens and users and hence less, rather than more, complaints. Advocating for timely appointments of tribunal members by the PCM will also contribute to reducing delays.

Transparency and accountability

Osinergmin places a high priority on transparent and accountable decision making. Osinergmin is committed to publishing all regulatory, supervisory, and normative decisions on its website supported by the raw datasets and other relevant non-confidential information used to render the decisions. It makes available raw data collected from industry on its website, and uses social media tools to disseminate information to a wide audience. It also publishes information on its activities, such as meetings held and a list of people met. Osinergmin proactively adheres to international standards and independent verifications for their management processes.

Different reporting requirements result in a fragmented flow of information going from Osinergmin to the Executive and the Legislature. For example, Osinergmin must send its financial information to MEF in the context of budget performance assessment. However, the PEI is overseen by the PCM. Reporting to Congress is sporadic: while Osinergmin can be called to appear before the Congress and its committees; at the time of writing, for instance, different parliamentary enquiries about high-profile corruption cases (none of them involving Osinergmin officials) are ongoing. However, the work of the regulator is not scrutinised on a regular basis and the regulator only engages with Congress on an ad-hoc basis.

The events linked to those investigations in Peru highlight the importance of strong mechanisms across the public sector to promote a culture of integrity, transparency and justice. Codes of conduct are a useful tool for regulators to define the informal and formal means of engagement with stakeholders, including regulated sector representatives, lobbying and interest groups. Osinergmin does not have an institutional code of conduct, but rather is governed by the ethical principles of the Civil Service Ethics Code (Law 27815). It is included in the Internal Regulation of Civil Servants (*Reglamento Interno de los Servidores Civiles*) of Osinergmin. Some provisions of the Law deal with conflicts of interest, but not with undue influence specifically. Osinergmin has been certified with anti-bribery international standards as detailed in ISO 37001:2016.

Recommendations:

- ***Advocate*** for more structured reporting requirements to both the Executive and the Legislature – for instance, reporting once a year to Congress, presenting and discussing the results of the regulator's annual report. Official channels can serve the dual role of providing greater opportunity for feedback, while also familiarising the administration and Congresspersons with the work of the regulator to alleviate concerns over a lack of technical understanding of the regulator's work. Regulators in Peru could co-ordinate in their request for more formal accountability channels building on existing legislative proposals.

- ***Strengthen*** Osinergmin's organisational policies in line with OECD recommendations on integrity, given the recent high-profile corruption cases in the Peruvian energy sector. This could involve building on the public sector-wide Ethics Code and adapting it to the role and functions of the regulator, ensuring that appropriate mechanisms exist to supervise internal adherence to the Code. Ongoing work towards the adoption of international certifications will support efforts in this area.

Output and outcome

Performance of the regulator

Osinergmin's strategic framework consists of the overarching Strategic Institutional Plan 2014-2021 (PEI) that sets out 15 strategic objectives underpinned by 40 strategic initiatives. There is little evidence that the PEI is used to drive the regulator's performance. The large number of objectives and initiatives in the PEI may be too large to empower Osinergmin's management to prioritise their actions and resources against those objectives. This also adds additional complexity to the monitoring of outputs since it does not indicate priority areas with respect to timing and resources.

In its current form, the PEI lacks some strategic components. While the areas included in the PEI are fairly balanced between input, the quality of the regulator's processes, and the output and outcome of regulatory activities (Table 4), the PEI's objectives are closer to a list of actions rather than of strategic objectives. The PEI is not accompanied by a forward-looking regulatory plan that would allow decision-makers to see trade-offs and synergies between objectives. The PEI does not contain a timeline for action. In addition, industry performance measures are not included as outcomes in the PEI but rather reported separately as part of the operational plan (*Plan Operativo Institucional*, POI).

The regulator assesses its performance through several mechanisms but these do not contribute to shaping and updating strategic objectives over time. Osinergmin assesses the PEI through an annual Strategic Plan Evaluation, a detailed document that tracks the number of initiatives completed and describes the actions taken by different departments. This measures performance mechanically, based on the amount and timeliness of internal projects completed, and places a lot of emphasis on the indicators of budget execution. In turn, the Board of Directors is informed about progress against the PEI but does not provide inputs to update the objectives over time.

The Strategic Plan establishes a key focus on improving relationships with external stakeholders but performance measures in this area could be stronger. While the annual reports include some measures of external reputation, all key strategic documents fail to integrate other important measures that track the performance of the regulator, such as the industry satisfaction surveys (EPERS). These documents neither reflect the results of the consumer research carried out by the Communications Department on social media interactions nor the fluctuations in the numbers of complaints and appeals.

Recommendations:

- ***Update*** a dashboard of performance measures aimed at enhancing the strategic drive of objectives and rationalising the number of initiatives. This can help the Board and senior management prioritise the most important initiatives and facilitate their ability to scrutinise the appropriateness of objectives and initiatives over time.
- ***Examine*** the quality of the regulator's actions in addition to their timeliness. For example, internal perception surveys to map the quality of service of different Departments could also be useful.
- ***Continue*** to map satisfaction and trust in the regulator through industry perception surveys (EPERS). Co-ordinate with industry and other supervisory authorities such as Indecopi who carry out biannual surveys on the reputation of various public organisations.
- ***Consider*** integrating measures of online interactions and user engagement, including at the regional level, in annual reports and performance monitoring. Additional performance metrics could include the number of user complaints and the amount of appeals, after careful consideration of the underlying reasons for fluctuations in these figures.

Table 4. Osinergmin strategic objectives according to the OECD Input-process-output-outcome framework

Indicator	Strategic objectives
Input : Efficiency and effectiveness of input (organisational and financial performance)	1. Use the budget efficiently. 2. Build an attractive organisation through the professional and personal development of its employees. 3. Have adequate information systems and technologies that provide support to Osinergmin's activities.
Process : Quality of processes for regulatory activity (existence and effective use of regulatory tools and processes)	4. Develop rules and processes, with autonomy, transparency and predictability for the business sector. 5. Serve the requirements of stakeholders in an understandable, quick and efficient form. 6. Integrate and improve the regulation, supervision and audit processes. 7. Strengthen communications with stakeholders. 8. Develop innovation and creativity through organisational learning and knowledge management.
Output from regulatory activity (effective regulatory decisions, actions and interventions)	9. Achieve credibility and trust of the society in the role of Osinergmin. 10. Monitor and regulating investment commitments in new infrastructure.
Outcome: Direct outcome/ impact of outputs (compliance with regulator's decisions) and Wider outcomes (market structure, service and infrastructure quality, consumer welfare, industry performance, etc.)	11. Promote the improvement of coverage at the national level of sufficient, affordable and quality services. 12. Encourage that the operations of the companies are safe for the community, workers and the environment. 13. Incorporate a long-term global vision in energy and mining that promotes the development of initiatives for a sustainable industry policy. 14. Promote decentralisation and linkage processes between consumers and companies. 15. Develop the conditions for regional energy interconnection.

Source: OECD analysis based on Osinergmin's strategic objectives.

Performance of the regulated entities

Osinergmin collects a large amount of data from the supervised and regulated entities but does not systematically assess sector performance. Osinergmin reports on the performance of regulated entities through a number of different channels including its annual reports and other sectoral analysis in its quarterly newsletter and statistical reports. The recently created Energy and Mining Observatory (OEM), available on Osinergmin's website, represents a sizeable step forward in the provision of integrated, accessible data and analysis for the electricity, hydrocarbons and mining sectors. This integrated approach is not yet reflected in the regulator's publications such as the annual report.

In the absence of comprehensive data management and systematic performance assessments, Osinergmin has not set overall performance targets for the regulated sectors. At present, different departments within Osinergmin monitor certain aspects of performance. For instance, the Tariffs Department has recently developed measures of service quality and incorporated those in price regulation models; the Osinergmin team administering FISE has developed numerous indicators of energy access in more remote regions; and the Mining Department collects detailed statistics on safety and the causes of accidents and incidents in mines across the country. However, the Departments do not set performance for the entities to achieve and Osinergmin's strategic documents do not present comprehensive targets for sectors.

Osinergmin is stepping up efforts to work collaboratively with the energy sector on performance issues. Osinergmin has been liaising with distribution companies under the National Fund for Financing Public Enterprise Activity (FONAFE, bringing together 10 public electricity distribution companies) to examine their progress and remaining challenges linked with reducing interruptions to electrical services. In addition, Osinergmin aims to share good practices for providing higher quality electricity services through a dedicated programme (*Mejora de la Calidad del Servicio Eléctrico*).

At present, Osinergmin reports performance through its dissemination channels using data at the national scale; however, important differences exist in sector performance across regions. In the electricity sector, there is a clear difference in performance between the privately owned companies operating in and around Lima and the public companies operating in the regions. This results in lower service levels (with more frequent and longer interactions) and lower investment (slowing down modernisation and interregional connections). The mining sector also faces a number of issues that are typically local in nature, such as the management of relationships between mining companies and the local population. Several extractive activities are currently on hold due to *force majeure* episodes, mainly caused by local protests.

Recommendations:

- ***Adopt*** a comprehensive approach to data management to avoid burdensome data flows and improved data interfaces with regulated entities, as the example of the Observatory shows. As regulators across the world adopt new approaches to managing big data, Osinergmin can build on its technical expertise and become a leader in this domain. Continued participation in international for a will be useful to this end. An additional benefit is the potential to develop market studies and foresight analysis in co-operation with regulated entities, allowing the regulator to have a reliable source of information to inform RIA analyses and to provide inputs to the policy-making process authoritatively.

- ***Streamline*** Osinergmin's approach to measuring performance and set high-level targets for the supervised and regulated entities. When performance issues emerge, this will provide a stronger rationale to demonstrate why and how Osinergmin needs to regulate certain sectors. Work with FONAFE companies on improving the quality of electricity distribution and the inclusion of initial performance incentives in tariff setting are positive steps in this direction. In addition, incorporating some sector indicators in strategic planning documents will show which outputs are directly influenced by the regulator activities and which are second-order impacts that the regulator can nonetheless influence through some of its actions.
- ***Renew*** the regulator's focus on local dynamics and issues. The persistence of performance issues in more peripheral regions of Peru points to the continued importance of strengthening the role of regional activities and in the provision of data, as 'ears on the ground' for Osinergmin. Better co-ordination with local governments would also be beneficial. In parallel, the regulator should consider publishing regional performance reports to better support the policy goal of bridging the rural-urban divide, which is a national priority, and evaluate progress in universal access to electricity.

Box 7. Market studies by the Italian telecommunications regulator (AGCOM)

The Italian telecommunications regulator (Autorità per le garanzie nelle comunicazioni-AGCOM) monitors market and technical trends. The agency collects information through questionnaires regularly submitted by operators. Key indicators are grouped under four categories: i) revenues; ii) volumes; iii) investment plans; and iv) employment.

These data provide a complete set of information available to policy makers and stakeholders, updated quarterly and published on AGCOM's website. AGCOM uses these data to analyse market performance and identify strengths and weaknesses in the Italian telecommunications sector.

AGCOM has implemented several web based systems, all fed by stakeholders' data. They include:

- *Informativa Economica di Sistema* (IES): this database collects demographic and economic data on the activities performed by operators, in order to collect information needed to fulfil legal and regulatory obligations (including, inter alia, market analysis, AGCOM annual report to Parliament, annual assessment of the *Sistema Integrato delle Comunicazioni*) and to regularly update the statistical internal data base.
- *Registro degli operatori di comunicazione*: this database collects information on the ownership structure of communications companies and allowing the application of media rules (anti-concentration thresholds, limits for investments of foreign companies etc.).
- *Catasto Nazionale delle Frequenze*: this database collects information on the use of the electromagnetic spectrum for broadcasting services (this information is used for spectrum management and planning).

- *Broadband map*: this database collets information on internet networks in Italy. This map offers users the possibility to search for information related to internet technologies such as speed and access in different areas, as well as the available telecommunications infrastructure. It is possible to search for 40 million geographical points; therefore, users can verify internet availability and speed even in small areas. The Italian broadband map has had almost five hundred thousand views since the beginning of the project in June 2017.

AGCOM uses collected data to prepare its annual report to Parliament. In addition, the agency provides data to the European Union broadband map project (www.broadbandmapping.eu).

Source: Information provided by AGCOM.

Note

[1] The system operator for the electricity market in Peru.

References

ACCC (2018), *Compliance & enforcement policy & priorities*, https://www.accc.gov.au/about-us/australian-competition-consumer-commission/compliance-enforcement-policy-priorities#the-accc-s-compliance-and-enforcement-strategy. [2]

OECD (2018), *Driving Performance at Ireland's Commission for Regulation of Utilities*, The Governance of Regulators, OECD Publishing, Paris, https://dx.doi.org/10.1787/9789264190061-en. [1]

OECD (2018), *OECD Regulatory Enforcement and Inspections Toolkit*, OECD Publishing, Paris, http://dx.doi.org/10.1787/9789264303959-en. [3]

Chapter 1. Regulatory and sector context

This chapter describes the main features of the sectors regulated by Peru's Supervisory Agency for Investment in Energy and Mining (Organismo Supervisor de la Inversión en Energía y Minería, Osinergmin). It also provides an overview of Peru's public institutions, and recent institutional and regulatory reforms.

Institutions

Executive

The main institutions of the Executive branch are the President of the Republic, the Council of Ministers, and the Presidency of the Council of Ministers (*Presidencia del Consejo de Ministros*, PCM). The Ministry of Finance (*Ministerio de Economía y Finanzas,* MEF) and the PCM constitute the core centre of government in Peru (OECD, 2016[1]). Together with the Ministry of Justice and Human Rights (MINJUS) they collectively have strong influence on regulatory policy in Peru. The Ministry with competences over all the sectors regulated by Osinergmin is the Ministry of Energy and Mining (*Ministerio de Energia y Minas*, MEM).

Figure 1.1. Structure of the Executive branch of the Peruvian government

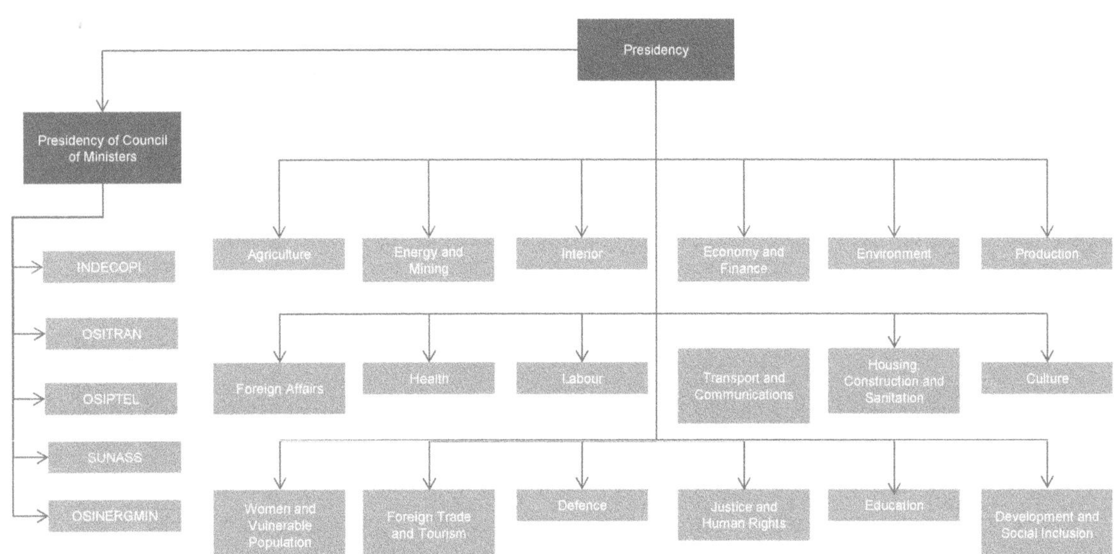

Note: The PCM also houses a large number of public entities, secretariats and commissions, which are not included in this figure.
Source: (OECD, 2016[2]), *Regulatory Policy in Peru: Assembling the Framework for Regulatory Quality*, OECD Reviews of Regulatory Reform, http://dx.doi.org/10.1787/9789264260054-en.

Presidency of the Council of Ministers (PCM)

The PCM is responsible for co-ordinating the national and sector policies of the Executive including line Ministries and public agencies. The PCM houses several secretariats and commissions, and manages and co-ordinates line ministries and public entities, as defined by law. The PCM oversees and provides guidance on the general administrative processes within Osinergmin and plays a key role in appointing and nominating the President and the members of the Board of the regulator, as well as administering budget allocations and disbursements. The PCM is developing guidelines and functions to strengthen its regulatory oversight role in the Peruvian administration. While not formally defined in law, the President of the Council of Ministers in practice plays the role of Prime Minister and government spokesperson (OECD, 2016[1]).

The PCM houses several public entities, secretariats and commissions. Osinergmin mainly interacts with two public entities: the National Centre for Strategic Planning (*Centro Nacional de Planeamiento Estratégico*, CEPLAN) and National Civil Service Authority (*Autoridad Nacional del Servicio Civil*, SERVIR):

- CEPLAN is a specialised technical body that is responsible for overseeing the national development plan as well as ensuring that sectoral, strategic, and operational plans of concerned government bodies are developed according to the National System of Strategic Planning (SINAPLAN, see Box 1.1). CEPLAN also monitors compliance and ensures that objectives and indicators set by the Executive are not contradictory with other sectoral or national plans.
- SERVIR sets human resources policies for the Peruvian public sector, including Osinergmin. It is responsible for orienting, monitoring, and managing human resource development, such as those relating to performance evaluations, information systems, remuneration, incentives and codes of conduct. SERVIR has authority nationwide, and over all entities and employment regimes. SERVIR has developed a new employment regime (see Box 2.3). However, as of 2018, no public entity has fully implemented the regime.

Box 1.1. Peru's National Strategic Development Plan (PEDN) and the National System of Strategic Planning (SINAPLAN)

In 2011, the government developed the National Strategic Development Plan (PEDN), which sets the strategic objective, policy guidelines, goals, and projects of the government for the next ten years. The plan consists of six strategic axes: "(i) fundamental rights and dignity of persons; (ii) opportunities and access to services; (iii) state and governability; (iv) economy, competitiveness, and employment; (v) regional development and infrastructure; and (vi) natural resources and environment" (CEPLAN, 2018[3]). The plan serves as guidance rather than a long-term action plan and provides flexibility in meeting goals in the medium-term by establishing annual goals every five years. The national plan was last updated in October 2015 and entitled as to include scenarios and targets for the country by 2021 (CEPLAN, 2018[4]).

The PEDN therefore serves as the National Centre for Strategic Planning's (CEPLAN) guidance for the application of the National System of Strategic Planning (SINAPLAN). SINAPLAN is an articulated set of systems and co-ordination mechanisms to assure the viability of and co-operation in the national planning process and promote sustained development in the country (CEPLAN, 2018[4]). Entities that make up the SINAPLAN include the three branches of government (executive, legislative, and judicial), autonomous constitutional organisations, sub-national governments, and the national forum that includes political parties and civil society organisations.

Source: (CEPLAN, 2018[3]), *Politicas y Planes*, http://www.ceplan.gob.pe/politicas-y-planes/ (accessed 22 June 2018); (CEPLAN, 2018[4]), *Qué es el Sinaplan?*, http://www.ceplan.gob.pe/sinaplan/ (accessed 22 June 2018).

Ministry of Economy and Finance (MEF)

The Ministry of Economy and Finance is responsible for the development and oversight of economic and financial policies in the country and plays an important role in regulatory quality efforts. MEF manages the performance-based budgeting system, which apply to all executive bodies and economic regulators, as well as other regulatory policy aspects related to administrative simplification, international regulatory co-operation, inter-governmental co-ordination, performance-based regulation, *ex ante* impact assessments of regulation and governmental transparency and consultation. It has the capacity to assess draft policies with potential impact on trade, along with other cross-cutting legal attribution (OECD, 2016[2]). MEF can also be consulted by Congress to submit its opinion on specific regulatory issues.

The *ex ante* and *ex post* impact assessments began in 2010 under the leadership of the General Directorate of Public Budget (*Dirección General de Presupuesto Público*) of MEF which directs, participates and supervises each of the stages of the evaluation process. Evaluated interventions can be activities, projects, programs or policies in progress or completed. To date, impact evaluations of public interventions of various sectors such as Education, Agriculture, Social Inclusion, Work, Citizen Security and Health have been developed[1]. In parallel, the Sub secretariat for Simplification and Regulatory Analysis (*Subsecretaría de Simplificación y Análisis Regulatorio*), it implements methodologies and actions for Regulatory Impact Analysis (RIA) in the regulatory training process, in the areas of its competence. It also issues opinions and advises public entities on the adequacy of the regulatory impact analysis in the regulatory training process.

Attached to MEF is the Agency for the Promotion of Private Investment (*Agencia de Promoción de la Inversión Privada,* ProInversión), which is a specialised technical body responsible for the promotion of investment in services and infrastructure through Public-Private Partnerships (PPPs). It provides information and advice to investors, mediating different views on investment projects, and creating a conducive environment for attracting private investments, in accordance with sectoral economic plans. Osinergmin is usually asked to provide a technical opinion on forthcoming PPP contracts. The opinions are published on the institutional website and, according to the regulatory legal framework, they are not binding. The final approval rests with the Ministry of Energy and Mining. However, if accepted, these opinions can generate modifications to the texts of the concession contract projects.

Ministry of Justice (MINJUS)

MINJUS acts as a legal advisory body for the Executive branch. It has a broad mandate to improve the quality of the rule of law and act as a legal quality check for draft regulations. Together with the PCM and MEF, it is considered among the most influential ministries in the Executive branch. It also ensures that the Executive branch performs its duties within the political constitution of Peru by providing legal advice and opinions on regulatory initiatives. It is also the agency within the Executive branch responsible for co-ordinating with the judicial branch, the public prosecutor and related entities within the judicial system.

Ministry of Energy and Mining (MEM)

The Ministry of Energy and Mining is the entity in charge of promoting the development of energy and mining activities in Peru. The Ministry is ultimately responsible for the planning and development of those activities, balancing the national policy objectives of attracting investment, meeting growing demand, promoting competition, providing a stable regulatory framework and protecting the environment in line with sustainable development goals (MEM, 2018[5]).

The Ministry is organised under three main departments, each headed by a Vice-Minister and a Director General: electricity, hydrocarbons and mining and each department is assigned specific functions. Some of the key powers in the area of electricity include: the approval of permits for new electricity generators; the oversight of PPP contracts; and the monitoring of progress against the national goal of universal access to electricity by 2021 in the context of the National Energy Policy 2010-2040 (*Política Nacional Energía*[2]), the National Energy Plan 2014-25 (*Plan Nacional Energético)* and the National Plan for Universal Access to Energy 2013-22 (*Plan Nacional de Acceso Universal a la Energía*).

Agency for Environmental Assessment and Control (OEFA)

The Agency for Environmental Assessment and Enforcement (*Organismo de Evaluación y Fiscalización Ambiental*, OEFA) works to ensure that economic activities in Peru are conducted without compromising the right to enjoy a healthy environment. Created as a specialised technical agency ascribed to Ministry of Environment in 2008, OEFA is responsible for the assessment, supervision, enforcement and sanctions in environmental matters, as well as for collecting information and applying environmental regulations in the mining, energy, fisheries and industry sectors (OEFA, 2018[6]). Until the creation of OEFA, Osinergmin used to be the authority in charge of environmental inspections and compliance in energy and mining. These functions were transferred in their entirety to OEFA in 2009. Similarly, to Osinergmin, OEFA is funded by industry contributions.

National Superintendence of Labour Inspections (SUNAFIL)

The National Superintendence of Labour Inspections (*Superintendencia Nacional de Fiscalización Laboral,* SUNAFIL) is responsible for promoting, supervising and verifying that employers comply with the national social and safety rules in the labour market. Created as a specialised technical agency in 2011, SUNAFIL is ascribed to the Ministry of Labour and the Promotion of Employment. Technical visits, studies and investigations are integral to the role of SUNAFIL. Until the creation of SUNAFIL, Osinergmin used to be the authority in charge of occupational health and safety in the energy and mining sectors.

Independent agencies

Regulatory authorities

Peru created four economic regulators and supervisory authorities in the 1990s as part of a broader policy built on the pillars of economic liberalisation, private investment attraction and regulated competition. These authorities exist today under the following names: the National Superintendence of Sanitation Services (SUNASS), the Supervisory Agency for Private Investment in Telecommunications (OSIPTEL), the Supervisory Agency for Investment in Energy and Mining (OSINERGMIN) and the Supervisory Agency for Investment in Public Transport Infrastructure (OSITRAN).[3] They were created to foster competition and promote infrastructure investment following the liberalisation of the economy. The defining features of these entities are: 1) institutional design as administratively independent bodies of the central government, 2) funding scheme through industry contributions, and 3) collegiate decision-making body.

Competition and consumer protection authority

The National Institute for the Defence of Free Competition and the Protection of Intellectual Property (Indecopi)[4] was created in 1992 as specialised public body in charge of enforcing competition law and intellectual property law.[5] Since 2010, Indecopi is also responsible for protecting consumers across the economy as the National Consumer Protection Authority, exercising its duties within the framework of the National Consumer Protection and Defence Policy, and based on four strategic pillars: 1) education, orientation, and dissemination; 2) protection of consumer health and safety; 3) mechanisms for the prevention and solution of conflicts between providers and consumers; and 4) strengthening of the National Integrated Consumer Protection System.

It has the authority to make binding decisions over sanctions or penalties and can fine up to PEN 20 000 for violations. Furthermore, since 2013, Indecopi has been conducting *ex post* reviews of regulations within their jurisdiction and has eliminated nearly 3 000 regulations in the country.

Indecopi chairs the National Consumer Protection Council, an inter-institutional working group created for the integration of the local and national statutory framework on consumer protection, as well as to bolster activities carried out for the benefit of consumers and to identify common information campaigns. The Council is made up of 16 representatives from the public and private sectors: ministries, utilities regulators, business associations, and consumers associations, in co-ordination with the PCM. At the time of writing, Osinergmin has been nominated to represent all other regulators on the Council.

Legislature

The legislative branch of Peru is conferred to the Congress. The Congress is a unicameral institution composed of 130 members elected to serve five-year terms. Its composition is the result of a reform passed in 1993 following the Democratic Constituent Congress that resulted in the new Political Constitution (OECD, 2016[1]). The Congress holds the authority to pass legislation that require regulators to develop secondary regulations. Furthermore, the Congress can call on the regulators for them to submit opinions on draft laws and to attend sessions to respond to any questions that raised by Congress. There are twenty-three (23) standing committees, including the Commission for Consumer Defence and Regulators of Public Utilities (*Comisión de Defensa del Consumidor y Organismos Reguladores de los Servicios Públicos*, CODECO), the Commission for Budget (*Comisión de Presupuesto y Cuenta General de la República*), and Commission for Energy and Mines (*Comisión Energía y Minas*).

Sub-national governments

There are three subnational layers of government in Peru: the regional government, the provincial local government and the district local government (OECD, 2016[2]). These government levels have exclusive and joint functions which are described in the Peruvian Political Constitution (*Constitución Política del Perú*, CPP), the Organic Law of the Executive Power (*Ley Orgánica del Poder Ejecutivo*, LOPE, the Organic Law of Regional Governments (*Ley Orgánica de Gobiernos Regionales*, LOGR) and the Organic Law of Municipalities (*Ley Orgánica de Municipalidades*, LOM). Sub-national governments have the authority to enact regulatory measures in their region. Osinergmin's decentralised offices (DO) are responsible for *inter alia* liaising with regional governments. Sub-national governments have the authority to enact regulatory measures in their region. Osinergmin operates 24 regional offices in charge of supervising services provided to customers in the downstream electricity, gas and hydrocarbons markets. These regional offices interact with sub-national governments on local issues including electricity outages and infrastructure emergencies.

Judiciary

The judiciary is responsible for interpreting and applying the laws in Peru to ensure equal justice. In this capacity, it is responsible for providing mechanisms for dispute resolutions through a hierarchical system. The judiciary is led by the Supreme Court and is supported by 28 superior courts with defined jurisdictions across the 25 regions in the country. Under each superior court are 195 primary courts responsible for each province and is then followed by 1 838 Courts of justice of the Peace within each district (Poder Judicial del Peru, 2012[7]).

Supreme Audit Institution

The Comptroller General of the Republic (*Contraloría General de la República del Perú,* CGR) was established in 1929 as the Supreme Audit Institution of Peru. As the highest authority of the National Control System, the CGR is responsible for supervising, monitoring and verifying the correct management, collection, and use of State resources and property. A comptroller general serves a seven-year term and is elected by a majority in Congress. It is represented in each government body, including Osinergmin, by the Institutional Control Body (*Órgano de Control Institucional,* OCI). The Chief Audit Officer of the OCI and is assigned by the General Comptroller of the Republic. Its function is the correct and transparent management of resources and assets of Osinergmin, safeguarding the legality and efficiency of its acts, as well as the achievement of its management goals, through the execution of control tasks, While the Chief Audit Officer of the OCI comes from the CGR. The rest of the audit staff are employed by the government agency. The OCI is responsible for all auditing all public spending; for example, by monitoring the procedure and evaluation process related to contracts, procurement, and other services.

Regulatory process and policy

Legislative process

Aside from the members of Congress, the President, the Judiciary, autonomous public bodies, professional associations, and the citizenry can submit draft laws to Congress for consideration.

Once a draft law is submitted, it is registered by the Congress document processing office of the Congress and processed by the Secretary General of the Executive Council, who is also responsible for identifying the committee that receive the draft law. The assigned committee deliberates and issues a report within thirty days and classifies it as favourable, unfavourable, or flat rejection. If more than one committee receives the proposal, they can submit joint or individual reports. If approved, the committee reports are received by the Executive Council, which includes the Secretary General, the Parliamentary Director, and the reading clerk, who will also be organising the debate and co-ordinating the distribution of the copies to the members of parliament. The plenary assembly then accepts or rejects the bill. An accepted bill is then registered, reviewed, and certified by the Secretary General's office and passed to the Executive branch. The President then endorses the bill into law and orders its publication, which then comes into force once published in the official gazette, *El Peruano* (Congreso de la República, 2017[8]).

If within its jurisdiction, regulatory agencies are entitled to formulate secondary legislations linked to the law, following the guidelines for the regulatory quality assessment of administrative procedures (Presidencia del Consejo de Ministros, 2018[9]).

Figure 1.2. Peru's legislative process

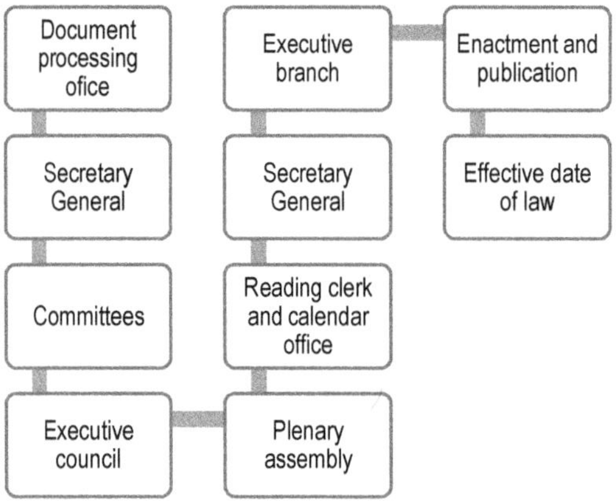

Document processing ofice → Secretary General → Committees → Executive council → Plenary assembly → Reading clerk and calendar office → Secretary General → Executive branch → Enactment and publication → Effective date of law

Source: (Congreso de la República, 2017[10]), *Legislative Process*, http://www.congreso.gob.pe/eng/legislative_process/ (accessed 26 June 2018).

Rule-making process in the executive body

The executive branch has the authority to issue subordinate regulations (decrees and resolutions). It is also responsible for approving bills (draft laws) that is submitted by the President to Congress, including any legislative decrees, emergency decrees, and resolutions, as defined by law (OECD, 2016[2]).

The rule-making process in the executive is not guided by a whole-of-government policy, but certain policies and framework serve as materials in the development of regulations.

Table 1.1. Frameworks and policies that guide rule making in the executive body

Name		Description
Law No. 26889	Framework Law for Legislative Production and Systematisation	• Sets the general guidelines for all regulated entities when preparing bills and other proposals, e.g. purpose and rationale (*exposición de motivos*). • Regulates the nomenclature, consistency of texts (titles, articles, etc.), and the management of errata.
Law No. 27444	General Administrative Procedure Law	• Sets important rules on public consultation, including the publication of proposals
	Reglamento	• Issued by the Ministry of Justice • Regulates the publication and dissemination of regulatory proposals and regulations
	Manual of legislative technique	• Issued by the Ministry of Justice • Provides legal guidance when drafting regulations

Source: (OECD, 2016[2]), *Regulatory Policy in Peru: Assembling the Framework for Regulatory Quality*, OECD Reviews of Regulatory Reform, http://dx.doi.org/10.1787/9789264260054-en.

When issuing subordinate regulations, the common practice among ministries is to draft a proposal, guided by the frameworks and policies outlined in Table 1.1, and posted on the website for public consultation. After consultation, Ministry or agency head approves the regulation. For ministries, vice-ministers would also need to approve the draft before it is sent to the minister. In cases when draft regulations require approval from three or four ministries and/or agencies, the proposal must be sent to the PCM to be discussed by the vice-ministerial co-ordinating council (CCV) or adopted by the Council of Ministers before it is sent to the President of the Republic for final approval. All approved proposals are published in the official gazette, *El Peruano* (OECD, 2016[2])

Box 1.2. OECD Regulatory policy review of Peru

In 2016, the OECD conducted a review of the regulatory policy of Peru to assess the policies, institutions, and tools utilised by the government and regulatory bodies in the country in designing, implementing, and enforcing high-quality regulations. This review formed part of the OECD Peru country programme along with xx other reviews of sectoral public policy in Peru.

The report provides an overall assessment of the political context of regulatory reform carried out by oversight bodies and relevant regulatory agencies in the country. It recognises the progress achieved to date, including the numerous tools and activities – such as a broad administrative simplification programme – utilised to improve the regulatory environment in the country. The report also highlights the challenges and improvements that remain in order to achieve a world-class regulatory framework and provides a set of recommendations and next steps, including:

- establishing a **regulatory oversight body**, as a way to create more coherence in regulatory policy activities and tools across ministries, agencies, and offices;
- issuing a **policy statement** – either through a law or a binding legal document – on regulatory policy, with clear objectives, strategies, and tools when managing the entire regulatory governance cycle;
- measuring **administrative burdens** created by formalities and information obligations;
- making **inspection and enforcement of regulations** an integral part of the regulatory policy framework, including through developing a set of guidelines related to ethical behaviour and corruption prevention;
- promoting a **coherent national regulatory framework** that actively encourages the adoption and use of regulatory tools and best-practice sharing.

In addition, the report provides a brief overview of the governance arrangements of regulators and their interactions with the central government. It underscores the degree of independence exerted by regulators on budget and decision-making, their transparency and accountability mechanisms, as well as an overview of the regulatory policy tools applied throughout the policy cycle. Economic regulators are considered to implement more sophisticated tools than other government bodies and have progressively improved its adoption and implementation.

Following the report, the Presidency of the Council of Ministers (PCM) has been proactive in developing initiatives and co-ordinating with ministries and regulatory bodies to improve the national regulatory framework. For example, in 2017, the PCM developed a set of guidelines for the regulatory quality assessment of administrative procedures to further improve the regulatory environment for citizens and businesses.

The guidelines aim to guide government bodies under their purview in identifying, reducing and measuring administrative burdens created by formalities and information obligations in both the local and the national level.

Source: (OECD, 2016[2]), *Regulatory Policy in Peru: Assembling the Framework for Regulatory Quality*, OECD Reviews of Regulatory Reform, http://dx.doi.org/10.1787/9789264260054-en.

Sector reforms and market overview

Energy

Between the 1970s to the early 1990s, the government of Peru aimed to develop the three main sources of energy supply in the country at the time: oil, gas and hydropower through public-led investment by State Owned Enterprises (SOEs). However the limited success of those policies led, in 1992 and 1993, to a series of major energy reforms broke apart state monopolies in the energy sector and introduced competition with private actors, including through the introduction of long-term concessions. Over time, Peru's oil fields continued to deplete although its gas production picked up substantially benefiting from private investment. Today, Peru is a net importer of oil and a net exporter of gas. Fossil fuels continue to dominate the country's energy mix at 81% of the total primary energy supply (MEM, 2016, p. 8[11]) although in recent years Peru has been aiming to develop more renewable energies, particularly at the micro-generation level.

Hydrocarbons sector

Peru shifted from being an oil exporter to a net importer in the late 1980s and early 1990s, following decades of dwindling production and investment in hydrocarbons sector. At the time, both oil and gas production were dominated by SOE Petroperu, which had been created in 1969 in a mass expropriation of reserves from both local oil companies and the largest foreign company active in Peru during this period - the International Petroleum Company (a subsidiary of Esso). However, declining profits and performance eventually prompted Petroperu to reinitiate a privatisation process in 1992. Underperforming assets were shut down or sold off, and Petroperu began to shelter its business decisions from political interference.

A new hydrocarbons legislation approved in 1993 effectively put an end to Petroperu's monopoly in the oil and gas sectors by allowing private companies to participate in every part of the sector. Prices were also deregulated. A number of improvements to exploration and production contract terms and the allowance of international arbitration in case of dispute helped attract new investor interest. Investments into the oil and gas sectors skyrocketed from USD 20 million to USD 4.3 billion between 1990 and 1997 (ASCOA, 2010[12]).[6]

Gas production, in particular, increased dramatically from the mid-2000s when the Camisea natural gas field, discovered in 1986, became operational in 2004. Situated in the environmentally sensitive Amazon rainforest, the Camisea field was estimated to hold 11 trillion cubic feet of possible reserves and 482 million barrels of natural gas liquids, making it the premier site for natural gas production in Peru, one of the largest energy projects in the country[7] and "the most important mega-field in Latin America".[8] In order to develop the Camisea field, the government opened tenders on various components of the Camisea project to attract international bidders. The first contracts to begin production in Camisea were awarded to an international consortium and is operated by Pluspetrol. The main pipeline carrying the gas from the forest to the coast of Peru was awarded to another international consortium led by *Transportadora de Gas del Peru* (TGP), while the distribution network across Lima and Callao is managed by *Cálidda,* whose majority shares are held by *Grupo de Energia de Bogotá*.[9]

Figure 1.3. Structure of primary energy production, 2016

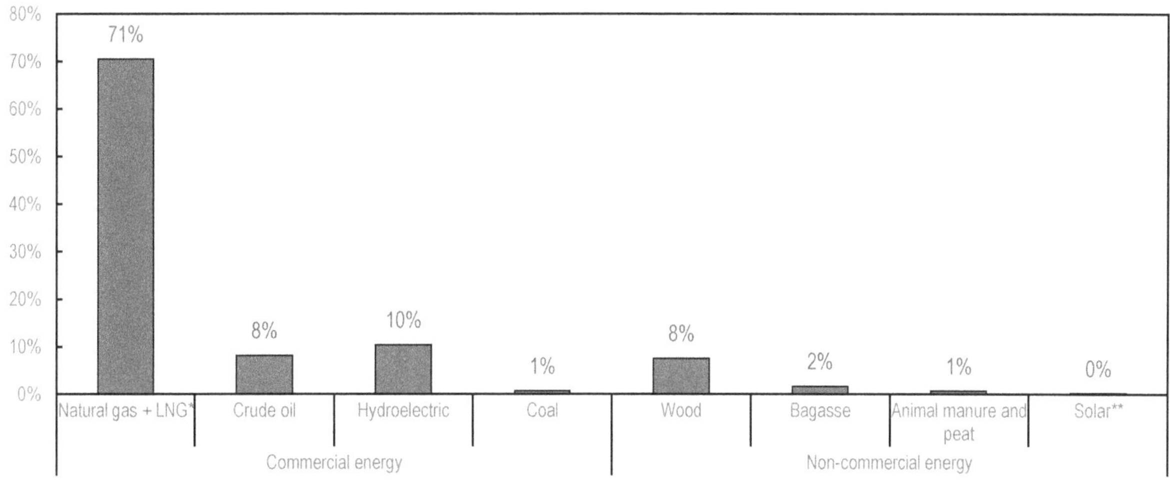

* Estimated. ** Taxable production.

Source: (MEM, 2016[11]), *Balance Nacional de Energía 2016*, Figure 2 : "Estructura de la producción de energía primaria: 2016", p. 5, http://www.minem.gob.pe/_publicacion.php?idSector=10&idPublicacion=565 (accessed on 26 November 2018).

Figure 1.4. Structure of final energy consumption by economic sector, 2016

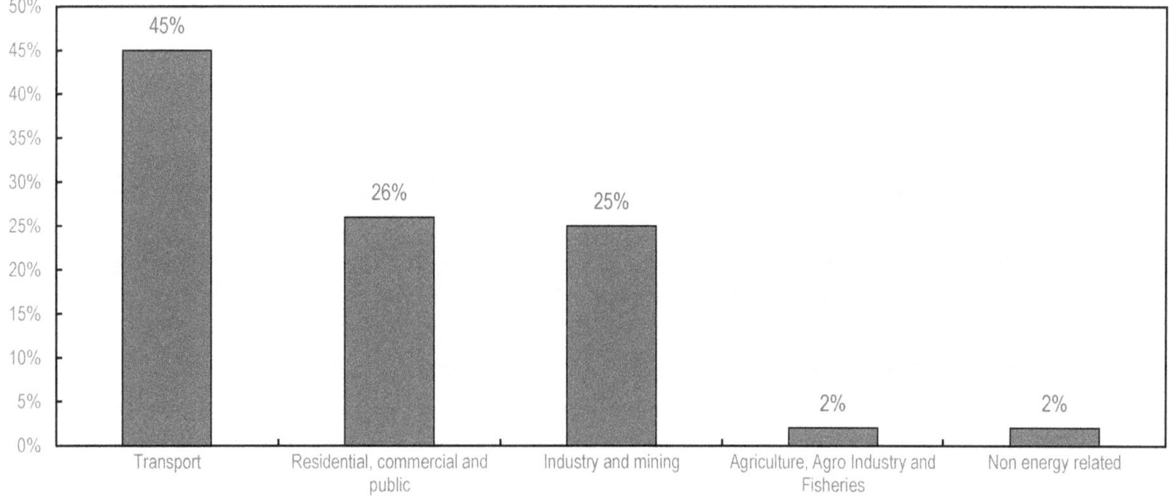

Source: (MEM, 2016[11]), *Balance Nacional de Energía 2016*, Figure 9: "Estructura del consumo final de energía por sectores económicos: 2016", p. 16, www.minem.gob.pe/_publicacion.php?idSector=10&idPublicacion=565 (accessed on 26 November 2018).

Today, over 70% of Peru's domestic energy production comes from natural gas and liquefied natural gas (LNG) and Peru is a net exporter of gas (see Figure 1.3). The government continues to support and promote the development of natural gas in Peru for domestic consumption as well as exports. By contrast, oil accounts for only 8% of total energy production, compelling Peru to rely on imports for oil and oil products to satisfy domestic demand, which primarily comes from the transport and residential sectors (see Figure 1.4). Several electricity generators use natural gas as their primary energy source.

There are currently four main Peruvian oil and gas companies: Petroperu, Relapasa, Pluspetrol, and Peru LNG. Many international companies are also active in Peru's hydrocarbon sector. Table 1.2 shows the composition of entities in the liquid hydrocarbon sector, supervised by Osinergmin. There are currently 44 hydrocarbons exploration and exploitation lots (Perupetro, 2018[13]).

Table 1.2. Entities in the liquid hydrocarbon sector

Type of entity	Operating units
Means of transport	22 885
Direct consumers of LPG and distribution networks	9 519
LPG service stations	8 704
Fuel retail station for vehicle use	4 886
Direct consumers of liquid fuels and Other Products Derived from Hydrocarbons (OPDH)	1 862
Wholesale distributors, importers and marketers	267
LPG bottlings plants	120
Installations for compression, transfer and decompression of natural gas	72
Supply and delivery plants	69
Direct consumers of natural gas	33
Producers and processing plants	30
Total	**48 447**

Source: Information provided by Osinergmin.

Electricity sector

Like the hydrocarbons sectors, the government controlled Peru's power sector until major reforms commenced in 1992. For some twenty years prior to reform, mainly vertically integrated SOEs Electroperu and Electrolima dominated the power sector since the 1970s. Electroperu served as a holding company for the various private companies already involved in dispersed, small-scale power generation. At the time, Independent Power Producers (IPPs) were generating as much as 30% of the country's electricity, primarily for own use.[10] However, the government was keen to achieve universal electricity access and to develop the country's vast hydropower potential, and Electroperu was deemed essential for both of these objectives. Electroperu thus came to generate most of the country's electricity.

Already in the 1970s and 1980s, to some extent vertical separation was present in Peru. While SOEs owned and operated power plants, various retail suppliers operated in different parts of the electricity sector. At this time, electricity tariffs were not adequately reflecting the cost of capital or production, and large investment projects – primarily in hydropower, which accounted for nearly 60% of total generation capacity in 1992 – had poor returns. By the latter half of the 1980s, Peru's power sector was facing many financial problems as companies incurred significant losses and reached unsustainable debt levels. Overall investment into the sector also dropped.

When electricity reforms began in 1992 with the Electricity Concessions Law and its regulations (Law No. 25844), the principle aim was to introduce competition and attract investors to buy up shares of the state-owned enterprises and run the power sector more efficiently. A Supreme Decree (No. 009-93-EM) followed in 1993. These laws and regulations essentially established the new structure of the power market with regards to generation, transmission and distribution activities.

Peru's electricity reform had four overarching goals:

- Unbundle generation, transmission and distribution under Electroperu and Electrolima
- Progressively introduce private participation and attract new investment
- Create a "free market" where large customers with capacity above 1 Megawatt (MW) could negotiate their own supply contracts
- Establish a new mandate for the Electricity Tariffs Commission (CTE) to become the energy tariff regulator and regulate prices based on marginal cost principles

The Electricity Concessions Law 1992 effectively unbundled the electricity sector and (while establishing Osinerg as an independent regulator, later transformed into Osinergmin). Electricity generation was divided into 13 companies, of which private companies accounted for the bulk of the generation capacity (70%). Transmission system was entirely privatised under six companies. The distribution sector, then dominated by state-owned Electrolima and 9 regional companies, was split into 16 companies (see Figure 1.5).[11] Electrolima's shares were eventually bought by distribution companies Edelnor and Elelsur, and power generation company Edegel.

Figure 1.5. Taxonomy of the power sector in Peru after reforms (2017)

Policy	Ministry of Energy and Mines (Long-term reference plans)	
Regulation	Electricity tariff Commission tariffs	OSINERGMIN Regulated tariffs
Generation	51 private generation companies 78%	6 public companies 22%
Transmission	16 private transmission companies 97% of lines >= 138 kV; 3% Other	
Distribution	6 private distribution companies 65%	14 state distributors 35%

7 222 693 regulated customers – 700 unregulated customers

State agency | Private company

Notes: kV=Kilovolt. The market share of generating and distributing companies is based on Mw.h.
Source: Data provided by Osinergmin (2017), "Gerencia de Regulación Tarifaria".

For all customers below the "free market" threshold, tariff regulations for medium and small customers were introduced. Transmission and sub-transmission tariffs are regulated either under a cost-based model (for existing assets) or as a result of a bidding process (auctions) for new assets based on Law 28832 of 2006. In response to rapid demand growth, the Law aimed to ensure the efficient development of electricity generation and reduce price volatility. To this end it mandated the use of auctions by distribution companies for the procurement of supplies to regulated consumers. Based on this law, Decree 1002 then established a mechanism were long-term guaranteed tariffs for electricity from renewable energy sources are auctioned biannually. Distribution tariffs have been regulated under a yardstick competition model, clustering companies under typical distribution sectors (e.g. urban high density, rural low density) and benchmarking them against the most efficient company of that cluster.

Figure 1.6. Organisation of the Peruvian electricity market

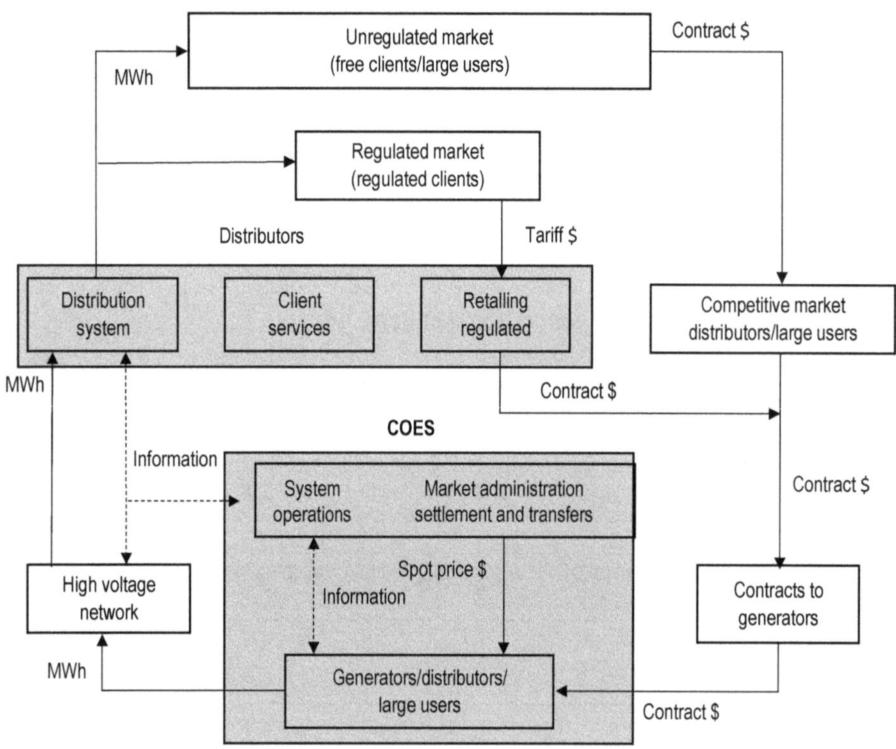

Notes: COES = Comité de Operación Económica del Sistema Interconectado; MWh = megawatt-hour.
Source: (Vagliasindi and Besant-Jones, 2013[14]) *Power Market Structure*, The World Bank, p. 209, http://dx.doi.org/10.1596/978-0-8213-9556-1.

A key outcome of the reforms was also the creation of the Committee of Economic Operation of the National Interconnected System (*Comité de Operación Económica del Sistema Interconectado Nacional* – COES), in 1994. COES brings together companies active in generation, transmission, distribution as well as large customers. Set up as a private, not-for-profit organisation, COES is governed by a shareholders' assembly of over 120 members and final decisions are made by the five Directors and, ultimately, by the President who is elected every five years. COES is funded by member contributions. The main roles of the COES are:

- System operation – following the merit order (least cost) criteria
- Spot market management – administering the short-term electricity markets by managing the gap between existing contracts and the merit order dispatch
- Planning – determining which transmission expansion projects should be given green light and providing opinions on new licenses and tests (pre-operative studies) as well as certificates for commercial operations.

At the time of writing, there are a number of both private and public companies involved in Peru's power sector (see Table 1.3). The largest companies supplying electricity to the market (ranked by MW of production) are ENGIE Energía Perú (7 807 093 MWh), Empresa Electricidad del Perú – ELECTROPERU (6 931 976 MWh) y Enel Generación Perú (5 877 817 MWh). All transmission companies are privately held and the ownership of 68% transmission lines is concentrated in the hands of 17% companies. Most distribution companies are privately-held. However, there is a significant gap in operational efficiency between private and public companies. For the year 2017, the System Average Interruption Frequency Index (SAIFI) for private companies was 5.8 interruptions per customer, and the System Average Interruption Duration Index (SAIDI) was 20.3 hours per customer. By contrast, SAIFI and SAIDI for state companies in the same year were 19.4 and 46.1, respectively. According to Osinergmin's analysis, he performance gap is most likely attributable to an investment gap, since public companies in rural areas have much more stringent financing limitations that constraint their ability to raise debt for investment.

Table 1.3. Electricity companies in Peru

Electricity companies	Public	Private	Total
Electricity distribution	14	6	20
Electricity transmission	0	18	18
Power generators	6	51	57

Source: Information provided by Osinergmin, 2018.

Overall, Peru's electricity demand has grown rapidly in tandem with its economy, increasing by more than 79% in the last ten years (COES[12]). The total number of consumers connected to the grid is shown in Table 1.4. Most of Peru's electricity demand is served by natural gas generation (55%) and hydropower (30%) (MEM, 2018[5]). The bulk of Peru's electricity goes to the residential and commercial sectors (40%), followed by mining (32%) and industry (25%).

Table 1.4. Consumers in the energy sector

Total number of electricity consumers connected to the grid

Type of consumer	Number
Regulated electricity customers	7 222 693
Non-regulated electricity customers	700

Notes: According to the Electricity Concessions Law, "regulated" customers refer to small retail or regulated users to whom distribution companies supply electricity at regulated prices. "Non-regulated" customers refer to large users (>2.5 MW) who contract freely and directly with generators or distribution companies. Customers between 0.2 -2.5 MW can choose between regulated or non-regulated contracts. Below 0.2 MW, contracts are always regulated.
Source: Information provided by Osinergmin, 2018.

Three major policy goals are yet to be attained in the electricity sector, as evidenced by discussion with key stakeholders:

- Universal access – ensuring that 100% of households are connected to electricity by 2022. Electricity access has already improved dramatically from 45% in 1990 to 93% in 2017, although a significant 20% access gap persists between rural and urban areas and an estimated 400 000 households lack direct access to electricity. Current efforts aim to extend access to around 8 000 households per month.
- Energy efficiency – renewed policy efforts by the Ministry of Energy and Mines currently involve an ambitious roll-out plan for smart meters within an 8-year timeframe and a requirement that operators reinvest 5% of their revenues in modernisation and efficiency-enhancing measures.
- Affordability – concerns about the inability of the poorest consumers to afford energy prices have been translated into action in 2003 when the regulator introduced cross-subsidies for one-third of the population consuming the lowest amount of energy. Further affordability measures are included in the wide-ranging Energy Social Inclusion Fund (FISE) scheme, as described in Box 1.3.

Renewables potential is significant but remains largely underexplored, in part due to very low electricity prices given the current mix and in part due to MEM is currently preparing to reform its renewable energy policy to facilitate free and competitive participation in the electricity market. The Ministry is assessing options such as introducing schedule blocks to tenders to help renewable energy producers target the time periods best suited to their generation profile.[13] MEM is also in the process of designing a regulatory framework to support the entry and utilisation of electric and hybrid vehicles.[14]

As of May 2018, Peru has 912 MW of installed capacity of Renewable Energy Resources in operation (RER 1st, 2nd, 3rd and 4th auctions); of which 39.9% are wind, 31.2% solar, 25.6% hydropower and 3.3% biomass. By the year 2020, renewable energy resources will grow with 360 MW of additional power installed (hydropower and biomass) MEM has announced a target of 15% of generation from renewable energy.

Box 1.3. The Energy Social Inclusion Fund (FISE)

The Energy Social Inclusion Fund (*Fondo de Inclusión Social Energético*, FISE) is a fund established in 2012 by Law 29852 to promote universal access to energy and a social compensation scheme for vulnerable and less advantaged populations. FISE is one contributor to achieving the objectives of the Universal Energy Access Plan 2013-2022, and includes the following objectives:

- Expand the use of natural gas by providing discounts and compensation for establishing natural gas connections in residential properties or promoting the conversion of cars from petrol to natural gas
- Provide compensation for extending the energy frontier to the use of renewable energy, including individual solar panels for households off the electricity grid and where grid expansion is not planned in the short-term. Expanding the use of energy-efficient lighting in residential and public systems is also included in this stream.
- Generate access to LPG to vulnerable sectors of the population via providing compensation (vouchers) for discounted purchase of LPG containers

- Ensure competitiveness of residential electricity tariffs by reducing the fixed charge, energy charge and other tariff options to eligible residential users via cash transfers to electricity distribution companies

The programmes under FISE are funded by large electricity users (mainly mining companies and large industrial players), natural gas transport service providers through pipelines, and producers and importers of fuels. The hydrocarbon and electricity companies are responsible for collecting these contributions and transferring them to the fund. FISE programmes benefit the most disadvantaged citizens.

The Law assigns the administration of FISE to MEM. The Ministry first transferred the management of the programme to Osinergmin through Law No. 29852, on a temporary annual basis. Since then, MEM has renewed Osinergmin's mandate every year, most recently until 30 April 2019. Osinergmin is responsible for the administration of the fund. MEM establishes and prioritises FISE's energy projects. Osinergmin's functions related to FISE include issuing regulations, enforcing sanctions, determining installation fees and setting the administrative cost incurred by electrical distributors for the implementation of FISE.

Source: Information provided by FISE, (FISE, 2018[15]), *Acceso a la energía*, http://www.fise.gob.pe/acceso-a-la-energia4.html (accessed on 26 November 2018).

Mining

The mining sector is a key contributor to the Peruvian economy. Mining exports amounted to 10% of GDP and 60% of the value of all exports in 2017, growing by almost 25% above 2016 levels. Over 30% of all foreign direct investment went to the mining sector. The sector employed over 187 000 workers and generated nine indirect jobs for every job created. In addition, 3% of all tax revenues come from mining. Peru ranks across the five top producers for the following minerals: copper, silver, zinc, lead and molybdenum.

For 2018, a total of 172 units belonging to 115 mining companies are supervised by Osinergmin. A mining company is defined as a company that has an exploration, exploitation, smelting and transport concessions. A unit is an area where mining activities are carried out or planned. Osinergmin only regulates what is defined by Law as a medium or large-scale mine.[15] For the smaller mines, regulatory requirements and inspections do not apply. Most of the large mines are located in the Highland Region of Peru. Due to the characteristics of the production areas, the companies, besides investing in the extraction and processing of the mineral, must consider the investment in the construction of mining camps, electricity distribution lines to connect to the national energy network, and access roads.

Table 1.5. Regulated mining companies in Peru

Categories	Total number of companies	Production units
Large-scale mining	37	77
Medium-scale mining	78	95
Total	115	172

Source: Information provided by Osinergmin, 2018.

The Portfolio of mining construction projects consists of 49 projects with a total investment amount of USD 58 507 million. Of the projects in the portfolio, three are in the construction phase whose start of operations is expected in the course of 2018. Likewise, it is considered that nine projects begin construction in 2018. It is important to note that 21 projects have a start date pending determination due to factors associated with business decisions and social issues, among others. This portfolio includes those projects whose purpose is the construction of new mines (greenfield), the expansion or replacement of existing ones (brownfield), as well as those of tailings reuse (greenfield). These projects meet three requirements:

- Investment (CAPEX) greater than USD 70 million.
- Start of operation or start-up in the next 10 years (until the year 2028).
- At least have or are developing their pre-feasibility studies.

In line with rapid growth in recent years, copper production is set to continue to expand. According to its main mineral of extraction, 26 projects are copper representing 68.6% of total investments with USD 40 155 million. Likewise, nine projects are gold and three iron, with investments of USD 7 120 million (12.2% of the total) and USD 6 700 million (11.5% of the total), respectively. The rest correspond to projects of phosphates, zinc, silver, uranium and tin, which together represent 7.8% of total investments.

Notes

[1] Ministry of Finance and Economy, "Evaluaciones de Impacto (EI)", https://www.mef.gob.pe/es/evaluaciones-de-impacto (accessed 23 November 2018).

[2] Approved by Supreme Decree No. 064-2010-EM.

[3] SUNASS was created by the Law Decree No. 25965 of December 19th, 1992; OSIPTEL by the Legislative Decree No. 702 of July 11th, 1991; Osinergmin by the Law No. 26734 of December 31st, 1996; and OSITRAN by Law No. 26917 of 23 January 1998.

[4] Indecopi was created by Executive Order No. 25868 of November 1992. Act 27444 and Legislative Decree No. 1256 serve as the legal basis for their methodology and approach.

[5] The only exception across all regulated sectors is telecommunications, where competition law powers rest with the economic regulator (OSIPTEL) instead.

[6] http://www.as-coa.org/sites/default/files/ASCOA_Energy_in_Peru.pdf.

[7] https://www.hydrocarbons-technology.com/projects/camisea/.

[8] http://www.pluspetrol.net/peru/camisea.php.

[9] The Group has also acquired a share of TGP (24%) in 2014, hence being involved at both levels of natural gas distribution (https://peru21.pe/economia/grupo-energia-bogota-compra-participacion-tgp-140924).

[10] https://www.ariae.org/sites/default/files/2017-05/DT13-OEE-OSINERG%20.pdf.

[11] https://elibrary.worldbank.org/doi/pdf/10.1596/9780821395561_CH09.

[12] COES – Estadística Anual – Evolución de la Producción de Energía 1993-2017 (GWh).

[13] https://www.pv-tech.org/news/peru-preparing-energy-reform-to-suite-renewables-minister.

[14] Ibid.

[15] Small scale mines covering an area of less than 2 000 hectares and producing less than 350 metric tons of output per day are not supervised by Osinergmin. This amount has varied over time:

- Legislative Decree 708 (06/11/1991): Up to 350 TMD.
- Legislative Decree 868 (01/11/1996/): Up to 150 TMD.
- Law No. 27651 (24/01/2002): 350 TMD.
- Legislative Decree No. 1040 (26/06/2008): Up to 350 TMD.

The limit of extension in hectares to small mining producers (Pequeño Productor Minero, PPM) has varied through time:

- Legislative Decree 708 (06/11/1991): PPM, those who have up to 5 000 Ha.
- Legislative Decree 868 (01/11/1996/): PPM, those who have up to 1 000 Ha.
- Law No. 27651 (24/01/2002): PPM, those who have up to 2 000 Ha.

References

ASCOA (2010), *Energy in Peru. Opportunity and Challenges*, http://www.as-coa.org/sites/default/files/ASCOA_Energy_in_Peru.pdf. [12]

CEPLAN (2018), *Politicas y Planes*, http://www.ceplan.gob.pe/politicas-y-planes/ (accessed on 22 June 2018). [3]

CEPLAN (2018), *Qué es el Sinaplan?*, http://www.ceplan.gob.pe/sinaplan/ (accessed on 22 June 2018). [4]

Congreso de la República (2017), *How does a bill become a law?*, http://www.congreso.gob.pe/eng/legislative_process/ (accessed on 26 June 2018). [8]

Congreso de la República (2017), *Legislative Process*, http://www.congreso.gob.pe/eng/legislative_process/ (accessed on 26 June 2018). [10]

FISE (2018), *Acceso a la energía*, http://www.fise.gob.pe/acceso-a-la-energia4.html (accessed on 26 November 2018). [15]

MEM (2018), *Ministerio de Energia y Minas - Institucional*, http://www.minem.gob.pe/_sector.php?idSector=10. [5]

MEM (2016), *Balance Nacional de Energía 2016*, http://www.minem.gob.pe/_publicacion.php?idSector=10&idPublicacion=565 (accessed on 26 November 2018). [11]

OECD (2016), *OECD Public Governance Reviews: Peru: Integrated Governance for Inclusive Growth*, OECD Public Governance Reviews, OECD Publishing, Paris, https://dx.doi.org/10.1787/9789264265172-en. [1]

OECD (2016), *Regulatory Policy in Peru: Assembling the Framework for Regulatory Quality*, OECD Reviews of Regulatory Reform, OECD Publishing, Paris, http://dx.doi.org/10.1787/9789264260054-en. [2]

OEFA (2018), *OEFA - Who are we*, https://www.oefa.gob.pe/en/que-es-el-oefa. [6]

Perupetro (2018), *Peru Petro Statistics*, https://www.perupetro.com.pe/wps/wcm/connect/corporativo/7a8738e6-be5f-4b66-9343-6ed107a87954/exploraci%C3%B3n.pdf?MOD=AJPERES&Contratos%20exploracion%20febrero%202018. [13]

Poder Judicial del Peru (2012), *Poder Judicial del Peru*, http://www.pj.gob.pe/wps/wcm/connect/CorteSuprema/s_cortes_suprema_home/as_Inicio/ (accessed on 25 June 2018). [7]

Presidencia del Consejo de Ministros (2018), *Guidelines for the Regulatory Quality Assessment of Administrative Procedures*. [9]

Vagliasindi, M. and J. Besant-Jones (2013), *Power Market Structure*, The World Bank, http://dx.doi.org/10.1596/978-0-8213-9556-1. [14]

Chapter 2. Governance of Peru's energy and mining regulator

The Performance Assessment Framework for Economic Regulators (PAFER) was developed by the OECD to help regulators assess their own performance. The PAFER structures the drivers of performance along an input-process-output-outcome framework. This chapter applies the framework to the governance of Peru's energy and mining infrastructure regulator (Organismo Supervisor de la Inversión en Energía y Minería, Osinergmin) and reviews the opportunities and challenges faced by Osinergmin to strengthen its performance.

Role and objectives

Osinergmin's mandate

Osinergmin is the safety and economic regulator for energy and mining infrastructure in Peru. It was established in 1997 as Osinerg with a mandate to oversee infrastructure safety and compliance with environmental regulations and occupational health and safety in the energy sector.

However, the role of the regulator has changed substantially over time:

- In 2000, tariff-setting powers for electricity prices previously carried out by the CTE (*Comisión de Tarifas de Energia*) were given to the regulator.
- In 2007, responsibility for supervising the compliance with infrastructure security, occupational safety, and environmental standards for the mining sector were transferred from MEM to Osinerg.
- In 2009, Congress (Law No. 29325) created an oversight body for environmental regulation, OEFA housed in the Ministry of Environment and in 2011 another body for occupational safety, SUNAFIL (Law No. 29783) housed in the Ministry of Labour and Employment Promotion. These bodies are tasked with overseeing a number of economic sectors in Peru.
- Due to the large changes in responsibilities and some unclear allocation of functions, Congress passed Law No. 29901 to better define Osinergmin's role as the safety and economic regulator for the sector while clarifying the roles of OEFA and SUNAFIL.

The executive has granted Osinergmin with additional mandates beyond its functions as the energy and mining regulator. As described above (see Box 1.3), MEM granted Osinergmin with the role of administering the Energy Social Inclusion Fund (FISE) under MEM's direction. The mandate was initially temporary, but has been extended. Furthermore, by means of a Decree (*Decreto de Urgencia*) in 2017, the Executive granted Osinergmin the additional function of nominating an assets administrator of the South Peruvian Gas Pipeline (*Gasoducto Sur Peruano*) concession after the original contract with the designated concessionaire failed.

Functions and powers

Osinergmin is governed by general rules that apply to all Peruvian regulators, as well as specific rules. Law 27332, Framework Law on Regulatory Agencies for Private Investment in Public Utilities (*Ley Marco de los Organismos Reguladores de la Inversión Privada en los Servicios Públicos,* LMOR) and Supreme Decree No. 042-2005-PCM (LMOR regulations) establish characteristics, functions and main organisational rules for Peruvian regulators. For example, the LMOR defines regulators as entities with administrative, functional, technical, economic and financial autonomy. In addition, grants them with general functions such as supervising, establishing tariffs, issuing regulations, imposing sanctions, resolving controversies and users' complaints (Figure 2.1). It also establishes the main Board of Directors and Users Councils (*Consejo de Usuarios*) rules.

Figure 2.1. Powers and functions of Peruvian regulators

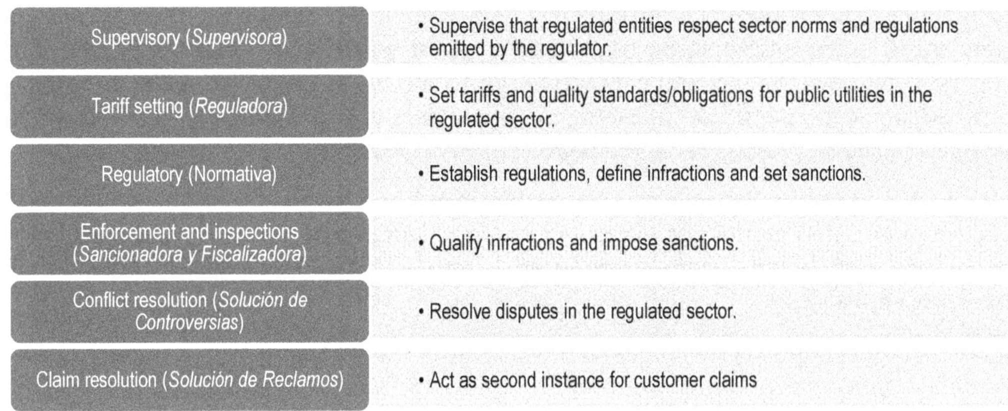

Source: Law 27332, Framework Law on Regulatory Agencies for Private Investment in Public Utilities (*Ley Marco de los Organismos Reguladores de la Inversión Privada en los Servicios Públicos,* LMOR).

In 2017, a draft law was proposed for strengthening the regulators functions and autonomy (*Proyecto de Ley de Fortalecimiento de Organismos Reguladores*). It has been discussed in the Consumers Defence and Regulatory Agencies Committee of the Congress (*Comisión de Defensa del Consumidor y Organismos Reguladores de Servicios Públicos del Congreso, CODECO*). However, it has not been discussed in the plenary assembly of the Congress.

The main specific laws governing Osinergmin's functions and powers are:

- Law No. 26734 Law of the Supervisory Organism for the Investment in Energy (Osinerg)
- Law No. 27699, Complementary Law of Institutional Strengthening of Osinerg
- Law No. 28964, which transferred the powers for the supervision and inspection of mining activities to Osinerg, making them Osinergmin.
- Law No. 29901, which specifies competences of Osinergmin
- Supreme Decree No. 088-2013-PCM, which approves the full list of technical functions under the competency of Osinergmin
- Supreme Decree No. 010-2016-PCM (*Reglamento de Organización y Funciones* – ROF), which approves its latest internal re-organisation and functions for regulation.
- Board of directors resolution No. 690-2009-OS-GG, which approves internal organisation and functions manual (*Manual de Organización y Funciones*).

Supervision, enforcement and inspections

Osinergmin's functions and powers are in regards to supervising the safety of infrastructure in the energy and mining sectors. As the supervision of environmental and labour issues is now the responsibility of OEFA and SUNAFIL, respectively, Osinergmin does not hold powers in these two areas.

In the hydrocarbons sector, Osinergmin supervises upstream activities related to the production and processing of oil and gas. For instance, natural gas activities include exploration, production and processing. The compliance with safety and technical standards for companies transporting natural gas is also supervised since 2018.[1] They also supervise the sole contract and concession for natural gas (Camisea to Ica and Lima). In downstream energy markets, Osinergmin supervises the compliance with safety and technical standards storage of liquid petroleum gas (LPG).

In the mining sector, Osinergmin is responsible for ensuring that mining companies comply with safety norms for infrastructure, installations and the safety management of operations. For instance, inspections look at the state of geo-technical, ventilation and transport appliances.

In 2017, Osinergmin registered about 49 000 entities to be supervised. During this year, 40 663 actions were carried out to supervise the technical and legal aspects (see Table 2.1). This resulted in 1 844 sanctioning procedures being initiated. Sanctions include *inter alia* fines, suspension and/or cancellation of authorisation for operation.

Table 2.1. Supervisions carried out by Osinergmin, 2017

Type of supervision	Number	Description
Pre-operational	17 773	Supervision program of modifications, expansions or construction of new installations.
Operational	19 506	Supervision program of operations and maintenance activities as well as safety of installations.
Special	3 384	Supervision in response to denunciations, complaints, emergencies and unexpected events.
TOTAL	40 663	

Source: Information provided by Osinergmin.

Tariff setting

Osinergmin sets wholesale tariffs for electricity generation, transmission and distribution activities, as well as natural gas pipeline network distribution. For hydrocarbon pipeline transportation activities, Osinergmin regulates only when the pipeline owners and the users do not reach an agreement. A competitive bidding process (auctions) is used to set prices for unregulated clients in the electricity market. Interconnection charges are also regulated.

According to the provisions of the sector law, the tariff setting process is carried out by first consulting with the regulated entities to request their estimation of the new tariff. Osinergmin takes these estimations into account and applies criteria and methodologies for determining the new draft tariff. This is then published for public consultation and adopted a tariff-fixing resolution, which is published along with the model for determining the tariff price.

In total, Osinergmin handles 108 different tariff processes. The tariff proposals contain relevant information on the historical and forecasted demand of the regulated service, the existing offer and future projects to cover the demand and the costs of investment, operation and maintenance of the infrastructure involved, among others.

Part of the tariff-setting process includes the requirement to consider return-on-investment (ROI) ratios to ensure the stability and performance of firms. Peruvian law established in 1992 requires the ROI ratio to be 12 percent, with a variation of plus or minus 4%. This was originally intended to provide stability for foreign entities to invest in Peru to expand significantly the energy system. Changes to this rate can only be made via legislative proposal by MEM, and only in 2% increments at any given time. The regulator has proposed reductions in the ROI, which have failed to advance due leadership changes at the executive level.

Cross-subsidies for energy affordability are also included in the tariff-setting process. The government created the social compensation fund FOSE as a cross-subsidy to reduce the bills of rural consumers so that they pay the same rates as urban consumers. Regulated entities have criticised both for transparency and ROI purposes, and in some cases have launched judicial reviews to re-examine the inclusion of cross-subsidies in tariffs. The Board of Directors handle second-instance appeals to tariff decisions.

In regards to infrastructure, Osinergmin has regulatory power in both electricity and hydrocarbon subsectors. In the electricity subsector, Osinergmin ensures the correct enforcement of the provisions of the Electricity Concessions Law (Decree Law No. 25844) and approves the procedure for setting the conditions of use and open access to the Electric Transmission and Distribution Systems so that it is in line with existing legislation and in order to avoid discriminatory conditions on the access and use of the transmission and distribution systems.[2] The technical standards and procedures to regulate those connections are set by COES.

For non-regulated customers, generators, transmitters, distributors or any interested entity, Osinergmin also establishes the procedures to request or make use of the transmission and/or electrical distribution systems for the provision of the energy transport service (Resolution No. 091-2003-OS/CD). In the hydrocarbons sector, Osinergmin regulates downstream tariffs for transport services, set every two years, and the distribution tariffs, every four years.

Osinergmin also promotes competition and innovative technologies in accordance with policies set forth by MEM. For instance, a recent policy from MEM requires smart meters to be installed within an eight-year time period and Osinergmin is responsible for implementing this policy objective through modulating changes in the tariff setting process in order to appropriately reward companies for the additional investment (Supreme Decree No. 018-2016-EM).

Dispute resolution

Osinergmin resolve disputes in the energy sector in regards to consumer complaints against companies or concessionaires, inter-company disputes, and disputes against their own regulatory or supervisory decisions. Should the claimant not be satisfied with the appeals handled by Osinergmin, a judicial review can be launched in the Peruvian court system. Osinergmin does not have responsibility to resolve disputes in the mining sector except for appeals against sanctions.

In addition, Osinergmin can issue directives to resolve complaints between electricity transmission and distribution concessionaires and third parties who wish to use those networks. Peruvian law requires that these concessionaires allow third parties to use these networks in exchange for compensation (Law Decree No. 25844).

Furthermore, the Transmission Regulation allows Osinergmin to issue a Connection Mandate to owners of transmission systems who refuse to grant access. Osinergmin can also set forth the conditions of access to the networks of the transmission or electrical distribution concessionaire when the parties have not agreed to the terms and conditions.

Co-ordination

Osinergmin operates within a complex governance system that requires interactions with several government agencies and departments with jurisdiction in the energy and mining sectors. The regulator provides its technical advice on matters of its competence and participates in co-ordination meetings when invited or issues reports when consulted. There are no structured co-ordination mechanisms with other public administration bodies.

Table 2.2. Peruvian public bodies involved in the energy and mining sectors or the regulator

Institution	Role	Interactions with Osinergmin
Congress	Unicameral legislative branch of 130 members.	Has the power to request Osinergmin to provide comments on issues or draft laws in either full plenary or in two standing committees – the Energy and Mining Committee and the Defense of Consumers and Regulatory Bodies Commission (CODECO)
Presidency of the Council of Ministers (PCM)	Co-ordinates national and sectoral policies within the executive branch	Oversees and provides guidance on the general administrative processes, key role in nominating and appointing Board members, administering budget allocations and disbursements.
Ministry of Economy and Finance (MEF)	Develops economic and financial policy for Peru, including co-ordinating the performance-budgeting system	Osinergmin must submit its budget to MEF and report on indicators to measure progress against the operational plan (*Plan Operativo Institucional*, POI)
Ministry of Energy and Mining (MEM)	Defines policies and strategies for developing Peru's energy and mining sectors	MEM established general sector policy, as well as performs some regulatory and supervisory functions. Can request Osinergmin to provide comments on issues or draft laws and regulations.
Ministry of Justice	Oversees judicial matters in Peru	Oversees the role of the courts, including the process of appeals and judicial review through which Osinergmin's actions can be challenged. Proposes an attorney general for all public institutions.
Regional Directorates of Energy and Mines (DREM)	Promote and supervise the activities of small-scale mining	While DREM supervise small and artisanal mining at the regional level, Osinergmin is responsible for medium and large-scale mining activities.
Agency for Environmental Assessment and Control (OEFA)	Attached to the Ministry of Environment and responsible for the assessment, supervision, enforcement and sanctions in environmental matters, as well as for collecting information and applying environmental regulations in the mining, energy, fisheries and industry sectors	Environmental supervision was formerly a responsibility of Osinergmin before being moved to the OEFA in 2009. Supervision functions in the energy and mining sectors overlap when accidents with environmental consequences occur, in the case of natural disasters, as well as regulations that affect the energy and mining sectors in both respects.
National Superintendency of Labour Inspections (SUNAFIL)	Attached to the Ministry of Labour and responsible for promoting, supervising and verifying that employers comply with the national occupational health and safety rules in the labour market.	Occupational health and safety was formerly a responsibility of Osinergmin before being moved to the SUNAFIL in 2011. Supervision functions in the energy and mining sector naturally overlap when accidents involving both infrastructure failures and labour occur, as well as laws and regulations that affect the energy and mining sectors in both respects.
Proinversion	Specialised technical body attached to MEF responsible for the promotion of national investments through public-private partnerships (PPPs) in services, infrastructure, assets, and other state projects	Can receive non-binding comments from Osinergmin when developing investment projects including on the quality and terms of infrastructure concessions.
Indecopi	Independent competition and consumer protection authority.	Has the authority to issue binding decisions and levy penalties on regulators or decisions taken by Osinergmin, as well as conduct *ex post* reviews of regulations enacted by the regulator and under the jurisdiction of Indecopi. Acts as consumer watchdog including in the energy sector.

Source: Information provided by Osinergmin.

Each entity has its own functions according to general and specific laws. The relationship between these entities should be governed by the principle of effective collaboration through agreements of inter-institutional collaboration to facilitate activities of co-ordination and mutual co-operation (Law No. 27444) In the case of conflict, the Law establishes the resolution as follows:

- Any controversy regarding competition between authorities of the same sector is resolved by the person responsible for it.
- Conflicts between other authorities of the Executive Branch are resolved by the Presidency of the Council of Ministers.

Osinergmin can be called upon by request from Congress, MEM, or other entities of the Executive branch to issue a non-binding recommendation on issues within their scope of competency. Two permanent committees of Congress are involved in the work of the regulator, including the Energy and Mines Commission that oversees the sectors and the Consumer Defense and Regulatory Bodies Commission (CODECO) that oversees regulatory policy more generally.

Indecopi requests non-binding opinions from Osinergmin with regards to competition and co-ordinates consumer protection with all the independent regulatory authorities. Since Indecopi serves as the national consumer protection agency and Osinergmin protects consumers in the electricity market, the two authorities must co-ordinate so that consumers bring their complaint to the appropriate authority. Indecopi has produced a guide to understand which regulatory authority handles each type of complaint to promote for efficient processing of consumer complaints.

ProInversion requests Osinergmin for opinions on Public Private Partnerships (PPP) contracts in the energy sector. When modifying PPP contracts, Osinergmin, at the invitation of MEM, participates in the joint evaluation process of the modification proposal, and issues an opinion on the modifications. The opinions on new contracts and modifications are non-binding.

The Government transferred environmental and occupational health competencies from Osinergmin to OEFA and SUNAFIL. Due to this change of mandates, there are circumstances where these three agencies supervise the same areas, regulated companies, etc.

The landscape of interactions between the regulator and other authorities is complex and the bodies involved often rely on informal co-ordination mechanisms. Occasionally, *ad hoc* working groups are formed to harmonise efforts. For example, a working group on electricity sector reform was formed in 2017 to review and propose updates to the Law on Electric Concessions in light of technological advancements in the sector. The working group includes the Vice-Minister of Energy from MEM, the President of Osinergmin and the President of COES.

International co-operation

Osinergmin establishes strategic alliances of mutual collaboration and co-operation with national or international organisations. The main objective is to contribute to improving efficiency in the fulfilment of institutional functions and objectives, through the exchange of established and agreed-upon benefits between the parties involved, seeking to promote energy efficiency and technological innovation. To date, 36 agreements with public organisations and 6 agreements with international organisations have been signed.

The core reason for these agreements is to create synergies to improve the efficiency of the institutional functions and objectives of the regulator, and contribute to the growth of the organisation. Specifically, they engage in:

- Information and experience exchanges in the energy sector;
- Co-ordinate the execution of joint operations within the scope of competencies to supervise the energy sector;
- Conduct bilateral training events to generate knowledge for each party;
- Conduct technical visits and exchanges of human resources to contribute to the professional, technical and organisational development of each organisation;
- Conduct joint studies and research in the energy field;
- Provide assistance and/or mutual technical support to carry out the implementation and maintenance of the tools and/or information technology support necessary to carry out the exchange of information;
- Optimise the use of both physical and virtual resources and contribute to eco-efficiency, within the framework of an interoperability and information security policy; and
- Contribute to the efficiency of both institutions by establishing co-ordination mechanisms to maximise human and infrastructure resources.

Osinergmin believes that these agreements have helped them to improve the use of good practices through the synergy of resources, implement professional development systems, and promote innovation through knowledge sharing.

Table 2.3. Agreements signed by OSINERGMIN with other agencies

Within Peru	LAC Region	Outside LAC Region	International bodies/fora
• INDECOPI • SUNAT • Judiciary of Peru	• CNE (National Energy Commission of Chile)	• K-Petro (Petroleum Institute of South Korea)	• ARIAE (Iberoamerican Association of Energy Regulators) • ICER (International Confederation of Energy Regulators)

Source: Information provided by Osinergmin, 2018.

With regards to international bodies and fora, Osinergmin held the presidency of ARIAE from 2015 to 2018 and the President of the Board of Osinergmin was recently elected Chairman of ICER for 2018-2021. Osinergmin contributes to these bodies more generally through its participation in working groups on energy-related topics. Additionally, as part of its commitment to ARIAE, Peru will co-host the Iberoamerican School of Regulation with Chile for two years. Osinergmin is also in charge of organising the World Forum on Energy Regulation to be held in Lima in 2021.

Osinergmin identified the benefits of participating in these international organisations and fora, as they provide an opportunity for them to exchange knowledge with other regulators. Osinergmin has also contributed to these organisations, including to a book on energy access in rural areas published by ARIAE.

Regulatory bodies do not have formal authority with regards to international agreements. Nevertheless, the Ministry of External Trade and Tourism (MINCETUR) who is in charge of negotiations sometimes invites Osinergmin to attend the relevant meetings and to comment on drafts of agreements.

Independence

The Peruvian regulatory framework grants Osinergmin, autonomy from the Executive. LMOR establishes Osinergmin as a public, decentralised organism attached to the PCM with legal status of internal public law and administrative, functional, technical, economic, and financial autonomy.

The Principle of Autonomy is further established by Supreme Decree No. 054-2001-PCM, which states that decisions of the regulator are not subject to mandatory instructions from any other body or institution of the State.

Osinergmin is a key player in the energy and mining markets, with a mandate to implement public policies, issue norms and supervise compliance with rules. Osinergmin mainly interacts with:

- The executive and in particular MEM as the responsible ministry for developing policies in the regulated sectors, and
- The regulated industries who need to comply with the decisions of Osinergmin and citizens, who are the ultimate beneficiaries of public policies and regulatory interventions.

The regulatory framework and the specific conduct of Osinergmin's management and staff determine whether such interactions strengthen or undermine the regulator's independence. Independence does not mean that regulators should operate in a vacuum, but rather ensures that its independent functions are carried out in connection and dialogue with other stakeholders.

Relations with the government

Osinergmin falls under the PCM who oversees all independent regulators in Peru. Any changes to the organisational structure, fees collected from industry, or communications with Congress must go through the PCM. In addition, the PCM reviews the PEI and POI of Osinergmin and appoints the members of the Board of Directors and of *Tribunal de Solución de Controversias*. Sectoral policies on energy and mining, however, are set by MEM, and Osinergmin is responsible for implementing them.

For budgeting purposes, the regulator obtains their funds directly from fees levied on the regulated entities and with additional no state budget. The funds are considered public funds despite being levied through private means. While the regulator considers itself to be adequately-resourced, Laws and Decrees passed by Congress and the Executive have an impact on Osinergmin's operating budget.

For example, recent annual budget laws have required all public agencies to return unused budget to the Treasury at the end of each financial year. This requirement applies to independent regulators, who must then make requests to MEF to use their unused funds for future projects (carry-forward balance). Additionally, austerity measures put in place in 2018 have placed restrictions on how the regulator can use its budget in regards to *inter alia* international travel, training and communications (see Input section).

In June 2018, the Commission for the Defense of Consumers and Public Services Regulatory Bodies (*Comisión de Defensa del Consumidor y Organismos Reguladores de los Servicios Publicos*, CODECO) of Congress discussed and passed a draft law to enhance aspects of institutional independence for economic regulators in Peru. The draft, which was based in part on OECD research, included measures to strengthen the regulators' administrative, functional, technical, economic and financial autonomy as well as their accountability mechanisms. As of November 2018, the draft law has not been proposed for discussion in Plenary.

In October 2018, MEM issued a decree that aimed at reversing an ongoing tariff-setting process by Osinergmin. This led to a conflict between the regulator and the Ministry, which eventually withdrew its Decree. Osinergmin could set tariffs on a descending trajectory as initially proposed, though as part of the regular regulatory process, Osinergmin reviewed the comments and data that supported them. The final tariffs approved reduced the extent of the tariff decrease (see Box 2.1).

Box 2.1. Osinergmin's 2018-2022 tariff setting procedure and Decree No. 027-2018-MEM

On 4 October 2018, the Supreme Decree 27-2018-MEM, endorsed by the Ministry of Energy and Mines, aimed to modify the methodology for calculating the Distribution Added Value (DAV), established in the Electric Concessions Law. This regulation added new stages and requirements that were applicable to the ongoing DAV setting procedure. The DAV applies to a four-year period and determines the distribution services tariff. The DAV has a direct impact on final users' monthly payments since represents around 30% of the final price for electricity services.

The DAV setting procedure starts by requesting the regulated companies for their new tariff estimation. Osinergmin considers these estimations to determine a new draft tariff, using the methodology provided by the Electric Concessions Law. Osinergmin publishes a draft determination and organises a public hearings for discussion.

Osinergmin published the draft tariff on 13 August, which implied a reduction of the current tariff. After this, Osinergmin carried out public hearings the 17 and 20 of August. During these stages, electricity distribution companies challenged the draft tariff arguing that Osinergmin did not take into account some necessary costs for providing the service. They stated that this tariff could reduce the companies' income by up to 20%.

At the time of issuing this Decree, Osinergmin was conducting the final phase of the process to approve the new distribution tariffs for the 2018-22 period in Lima, Callao and Ica. The expected conclusion of the process was 16 October 2018, with new tariffs entering into force from 1st November.

On 5 October, Osinergmin issued a public statement rejecting the Decree arguing that it affected the independence of the regulator. Given the importance of the regulations, Osinergmin considered that the Decree should have been discussed or pre-published for comments. Osinergmin's concerns were backed by the Iberoamerican Association of Energy Regulators (ARIAE) with a public statement deploring the interventionist approach of the Peruvian government.

On 4 October, the Supreme Decree 28-2018-EM revoked the original Decree whilst Osinergmin was finishing the ongoing DAV calculation procedure. On 16 October, Osinergmin published the new electricity tariffs for Lima, Callao and Ica, which will apply from 1st November 2018 to 31st October 2022. The final tariffs represent a 1.6% to 4.3% reduction.

Source: Information provided by Osinergmin, 2018.

Relations with the regulated sector

Market players, who trust the level of expertise and autonomy displayed by both senior and technical staff, regard Osinergmin as a highly technical institution.

Osinergmin carries out public consultations for draft regulations related to tariff-setting. Osinergmin publishes these drafts and organises public hearings for stakeholders For the purpose of transparency, a comments matrix is published with the final regulation that shows the comments made by stakeholders and the regulator's response.

Early stage consultation is rarely used when developing new measures, particularly new technical norms and standards. LMOR requires Users Councils, including representatives from industrial associations. However, the regulator has not been able to rely on inputs from the Council in recent years. Other regulatory agencies have noted similar problems in their relationship with Users Councils in Peru.

In order to improve its communication with stakeholders, Osinergmin has set this as a priority in their strategic plan, while also fostering a culture of transparency on regulatory decisions through Regulatory Impact Analyses and adhering to international regulatory quality management standards (ISO 9001).

Independence and legitimacy in regulatory decisions is enhanced through the development of technical regulatory tools such as demand studies, incremental cost models, regulatory accounting systems, statistics processing systems, tariff registration systems and support from high-level consultancy firms. Osinergmin also actively publish and disseminates reports, including investigative reports, reports with academia, and issuing of periodic bulletins.

Strategic and operational objectives

The Government of Peru establishes the strategic goals for the energy sector and ensures an appropriate framework is in place to enable delivery. Two documents set out the government's policy goals in relation to energy and mining: the National Energy Plan 2014-2025 and the National Energy Policy 2010-2040. The regulator plays a crucial role in ensuring that these objectives can be attained.

The Government requires the regulator to develop a Strategic Institutional Plan (*Plan Estratégico Institucional,* PEI) as the main reference framework for the management of its internal activities. Osinergmin's current PEI runs from 2015 to 2021. Previously, four-year plans were produced but the current PEI was extended to seven years for to incorporate the vision of the future for the Peruvian State for the year 2021.

The Planning, Budget and Modernisation Department (GPPM) is responsible for co-ordinating and drafting the strategic objectives, which are developed in line with the main objectives, mission and vision of the organisation. Under the auspices of the

General Manager, the GPPM then presents the PEI to the President of the Board of Directors for final approval before publication.

Box 2.2. Osinergmin's mission

Osinergmin's mission is currently defined as follows:

- "To regulate, oversee and supervise the energy and mining sectors with autonomy, technical capacity, clear and predictable rules, in order for activities in these sectors to develop safely and with the goal of having a reliable and sustainable energy supply" (PEI 2015-2021, p.8).

The values of commitment, excellence, service, integrity and autonomy underpin the rest of the strategic plan and culminate in Osinergmin's value proposition:

- "Be proactive to ensure that Peru counts on adequate, reliable, accessibility and quality energy services covering the national territory. Ensure that companies working in the energy and mining sectors run their activities in a manner that is safe for the community, workers and the environment.
- Provide to investors and funders a regulatory and a supervisory framework with clear and predictable rules that allows them to achieve adequate returns and incentivises further investment.
- Implement or ensure the implementation of sectoral energy and mining policies, offering public institutions technical and foresight support, allowing them to promote sustainable sectoral policies and having adequate information to achieve their functions.
- Create an innovative institution, built on competent and motivated employees, working in an attractive and challenging environment that promotes and strengthens their personal and professional development."

Source: PEI 2015-2021, p. 8.

The PEI is developed in dialogue with both external stakeholders and internal teams. External stakeholders include citizens, regulated entities, and other government institutions, including the PCM, MEM, INDECOPI, the Ombudsman (*Defensoría del Pueblo*), National Institute of Quality (*Inacal*), and Congress. Participation is through a survey with each external community that asks how the regulator is perceived, how they are helping the sector, and how they are performing in the relationship with each relevant stakeholder.

Internally, a variety of participants are included via the Strategic Planning Committee, composed of 23 individuals, members of the Board of Directors (including the President), the General Manager, and working groups for each sector composed of, on average, seven individuals each. In addition, Osinergmin organises group workshops, one with Osinergmin employees and two with supervisors to understand their perception of Osinergmin development with respect to various aspects of its mandate.

The 2015-21 PEI includes 15 strategic objectives based on four perspectives: stakeholders; internal processes; human sources development, learning and technology; and financial resources (see Table 2.4). This is accompanied by 40 initiatives and

30 indicators (the full breakdown of the PEI can be found in Annex 2.A). The PEI is implemented through yearly operational plans (*Plan Operativo Instituciónal,* POI) and underpinned by a three-year budget. Each year, the budget is reviewed and projections are revised and re-approved. A management model is built based on these indicators and used each year to communicate to the staff the results of the prior year, the strategic objectives for the new year and assign resources and responsibilities to achieve these goals (see Output and outcome section).

Table 2.4. Osinergmin Strategic Institutional Objectives 2014-21

Category of focus		Strategic objective
Stakeholders	1.	Achieve credibility and trust of the society in the role of Osinergmin
	2.	Develop rules and processes, with autonomy, transparency and predictability for the business sector
	3.	Promote the improvement of coverage at the national level of sufficient, affordable and quality services
	4.	Serve the requirements of stakeholders in an understandable, quick and efficient form
	5.	Encourage that the operations of the companies are safe for the community, workers and the environment
Internal processes	1.	Integrate and improve the regulation, supervision and audit processes
	2.	Incorporate a long-term global vision in energy and mining that promotes the development of initiatives for a sustainable industry policy
	3.	Promote decentralisation and linkage processes between consumers and companies
	4.	Strengthen communications with stakeholders
	5.	Develop the conditions for regional energy interconnection
	6.	Monitoring and regulating investment commitments in new infrastructure
Human resources development, learning and technology	1.	Develop innovation and creativity through organisational learning and knowledge management
	2.	Build an attractive organisation through the professional and personal development of its employees
	3.	Have adequate information systems and technologies that provide support to OSINERGMIN's activities
Financial resources	1.	Use the budget efficiently

Source: Information provided by Osinergmin, 2018.

The PEI 2015-21 was developed based on the *Modelo Iberoamericano de Excelencia en la Gestion* developed by the *Fundibeq* as an international standard. A Balance Scorecard Methodology was used to develop strategic objectives and measures. Since 2015, CEPLAN (the central authority responsible for overseeing the National Development Plan) have established a common methodology for public sector entities and the new plans by Osinergmin after 2021 will need to reflect CEPLAN's indications. This will provide an incentive to review and update the current performance measures. For example, CEPLAN requires that indicators be developed to measure progress towards objectives and ensure that these indicators are properly justified; CEPLAN also issued new guidelines for developing institutional plans that require more information regarding the impacts on the population and geographic effects, i.e. urban versus rural affects.

Input

Financial resources

The contribution rate from industry is approved by the Executive through a Supreme Decree endorsed by the President of the Council of Ministers and MEF[3] and cannot exceed 1% of the total annual income of regulated firms after taxes[4] of each firm, minus GST and MPT. For mining, the contribution rate is limited to large- and medium-scale mining entities, as defined according to the economic impact of all mining operations under one firm.

Contributions constitute 90% of Osinergmin's total budget. Additional revenue can be collected from (OECD, 2016[1]):

- Payments from administrative procedures enlisted in their Single Text of Administrative Processes (*Texto Único de Procedimientos Administrativos*, TUPA)
- Donations, contributions or transfers made by natural or legal, national or international persons. Interests or late fees derived from the regulatory contribution
- Financial interests generated by their own resources
- Sources from fines

The regulatory contribution rate is determined *ex ante* based on revenue projections of the regulated sectors rather than determined in accordance with a cost recovery principle. Since 2013, Osinergmin proposes three-year period rates for the energy and mining sectors. Table 2.5 provides an overview of regulatory contributions for 2017-19. These decrease marginally to respond to industry concerns that rates are too high.

Table 2.5. Rate of regulatory contributions to Osinergmin, 2017-19

Sector	Rate of regulatory contribution (% of annual income)		
	2017	2018	2019
Electricity	0.52%	0.51%	0.50%
Hydrocarbons			
• Import and production of fuels, including liquefied petroleum gas (LPG) and natural gas (LNG)	0.36%	0.35%	0.34%
• Concessionaires of hydrocarbons transport and distribution via pipelines	0.57%	0.56%	0.55%
Mining	0.15%	0.14%	0.13%

Source: Information provided by Osinergmin, 2018.

Funds collected from fines and sanctions, as well as some annual contributions, are transferred in various rates to national development funds. In the case of the energy sector, monthly collections are transferred entirely to the Rural Electrification Fund managed by MEM. For the Mining Sector, 30% of annual revenue is transferred to the Regional Directorates of Energy and Mines (DREMs) which supervise small-scale mining in Peru.

Osinergmin considers funds are enough to meet its needs. However, recent changes to budget laws have imposed limits on regulators to fully use its budget. Since the regulator is funded solely through contributions collected directly from regulated entities, their funds are classified as "directly collected resources" (RDR), and not "ordinary resources" (OR) collected from taxes that mostly fund the operation of regular government entities. Some government entities can also have RDR funds, i.e. police who collect fines.

National budget law previously allowed agencies with RDR funds to keep surplus funds and carry them forward to future spending, while agencies with OR funds were required to return surpluses to the Treasury each year. For the 2017 fiscal year, MEF issued the Law of Financial Equilibrium (*Ley de Equilibrio Financiero*), which required that surplus RDR funds to also be forwarded to the Treasury in order to promote higher budget execution across public entities. Exceptions are made for natural disaster financing, sanitary measures, or funds committed to multi-year investment processes.

To date, Osinergmin surpluses have been forwarded to the national treasury to finance public expenditures not related to the regulated industries. This provision must be renewed yearly with the national budget law. Forwarding surpluses was renewed for the 2018 fiscal year and is expected to be renewed for 2019. Table 2.6 provides an overview of Osinergmin's annual budget, as well as its execution annual percentage over the last four years.

Table 2.6. Osinergmin annual budget and execution, 2015-18

Year	2015	2016	2017	2018
Budget (million PEN)	328.5	349.5	402.6	410.8
• Contributions	326.7	331.2	358.5	373.3
• Sales of Goods and services	1.8			
• Interest		3.3	11.5	15.5
• Fines	0	15	32.6	19.8
• Current Account Balance				2.2
Execution (%)	90.9%	89.5%	77.7%	34.3%

Note: Budget execution for 2018 is as of May 2018.
Source: Information provided by Osinergmin, 2018.

Managing financial resources

Osinergmin produces a three-year budget that aligns technical analysis and decision-making on the priorities indicated in the PEI/POI, their initiatives and goals, which are expected to be carried out for the achievement of the objectives. This is implemented through annual budgets that include the Annual Supervision Plan and various elements of the Process Management. Osinergmin produces a strategic map to align these objectives and performance measures with the budget. These initiatives, which in some cases are multiannual, are carried out over shorter periods to facilitate the monitoring and evaluation of the results. The multi-annual budget is reviewed yearly to allow for updates and corrections as needed and renewed for a further three-year period.

The PCM, through Supreme Decree, established the guidelines and methodology for the Process Management to elaborate the competencies and responsibilities assigned to each entity. The Process Management specifically elaborates three levels of documents that must be established: Process Map (PM), Processes and Procedures Manual (MGPP), and specific procedures (MAPROS).

The Process Map of the institution identifies the strategic, operational and support processes for the electricity, natural gas, liquid hydrocarbon and mining sectors. Process management includes the identification of the needs and expectations of the stakeholders, the implementation, the measurement of satisfaction and feedback. One of the key requirements for the processes is the allocation of budget to cover the operating costs and achieve compliance with their strategic objectives. The budget process is co-ordinated with the national government digitally through a system linked with MEF, which is the same system for all government agencies.

The process for creating the budget is accomplished through five stages:

- **Planning**: Osinergmin estimate revenues to be collected, and forecasts costs and investments to be executed based on the PEI and POI. Rules are set by MEF.
- **Formulation**: Osinergmin prioritise goals and aligns them with functions and financing. MEF establishes the rules. Planning and formulation is completed by May each year, and defended to the MEF by July to begin the approvals process.
- **Approval**: Osinergmin approve the Opening Institutional Budget, according to the amounts authorised in the Budget Law by 31 December. MEF establishes the rules, receives budget proposals and schedules meetings to review supporting information. MEF consolidates proposals, which is approved by the Council of Ministers and sent to Congress by 30 August of each year. Congress Budget Commission scrutinises the budgets with MEF and the Ministers, including calling on the heads of public entities to ask questions. The Congress approves the Budget Law by 30 November and sends it to the Executive. The Executive must publish the Budget Law no later than 15 days after Congress signs off.
- **Execution**: Osinergmin execute the budget between 1 January and 31 December each year. MEF establishes the rules for implementation and receives the approval resolutions of institutional budgets that each entity has to issue within five days of the approval of the institutional budget. Congress oversees the budget execution, also receiving the approval resolutions of the institutional budgets within five days of approval.
- **Evaluation**: Osinergmin evaluate the budget execution at the level of goals achieved, tracking what goals have been achieved and using how much of the budget. MEF establishes the rules of semi-annual and annual evaluation. Evaluations occur in April and June each year.

Managers carry out reviews of their budgetary balances. The digital management system (SAI) produces a Funds Control Consultation report that allows Managers to visualise their expenses by level and phases (Commitment, Pre Commitment, Accrued and Revolved). To determine budgetary modifications, they can make budgetary transfers through the SAI that are approved according to the procedures. The GPPM is responsible for updating manually the information that is not automatically interfaced with SIA system.

In 2015, the Government of Peru implemented a performance budgeting system for all government entities and managed by MEF. MEF requires budgets to be aligned with the goals and objectives established by the institution in their PEI and POIs. The goal is to ensure agencies consider the problems they are trying to solve and have measurable indicators of success towards solving these problems. MEF works with the various government agencies to help design better indicators by encouraging them to follow the methodology and develop indicators that show how institutional actions are leading to positive improvements in the sector and for society. MEF does not comment on the appropriateness of the indicators, simply the process.

Osinergmin has begun implementing the performance budgeting system over the last two years (see Figure 2.2).

Figure 2.2. Osinergmin results-based budget process

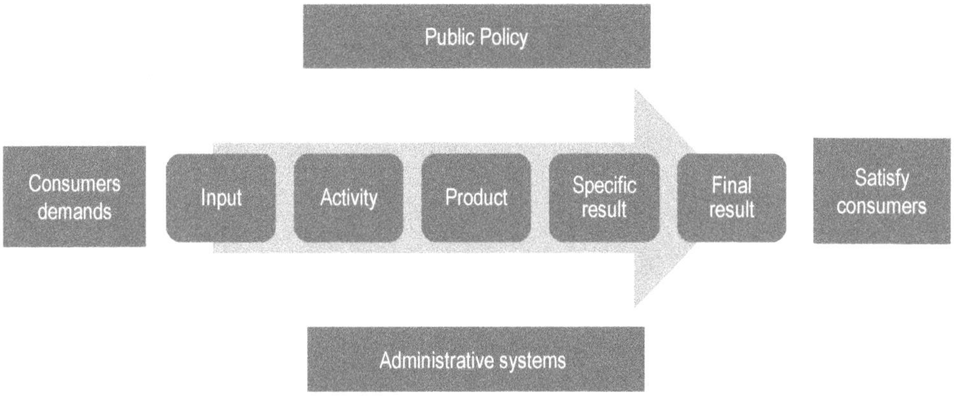

Source: Information provided by Osinergmin.

Performance budgeting is implemented through budget programmes, performance monitoring actions based on indicators, evaluations and management incentives determined by MEF. The general rules for the budgeting process are issued by MEF, to which all the entities that make up the public sector are subject, from the three levels of government: national, regional and local. Osinergmin is part of the national government entities.

Human resources

Osinergmin employs 687 staff as of June 2018. The increase in staff in recent years is mainly the result of new tasks given to Osinergmin and the decision to strengthen the decentralisation of activities in the regional offices. New recruits for the dispute resolution bodies and to support the roll out of RIA have also joined.

Osinergmin has an Organisation and Functions Manual (*Manuel de Organización y Funciones*), which outlines the main functions and responsibilities of the positions within the organisation and describes the professional profile required for each position. The posts are approved by the President of the Board. A full breakdown by job family of the professional staff can be found in Table 2.8.

Table 2.7. Osinergmin staff by category, 2014-18

Year	Number of support staff	Number of professional staff	Total workforce
2018	103	584	687
2017	92	568	660
2016	89	542	631
2015	93	474	567
2014	77	427	504

Source: Information provided by Osinergmin, 2018.

Table 2.8. Osinergmin professional staff by category, 2018

Job family/profession	2018
Accounting	30
Communications	17
Economics	49
Legal	121
Managerial	33
Planning and Budget	6
Engineering	280
Information technology	38
Other	16

Note: All categories of staff other than support staff are considered professional staff.
Source: Information provided by Osinergmin, 2018.

Table 2.9. Female/Male staff by category, 2018

Category	Female	Male
Senior management (Chairperson, manager, and advisors)	5	15
Technical staff	159	405
Support staff	66	37
TOTAL	230	457

Source: Information provided by Osinergmin, 2018.

Osinergmin's public servants work under two different employment regimes. Some employees (37%) work under labour regulations for the private sector, not commonly offered in public entities (Law 728 regime), and other employees (63%) work under non-permanent positions (Law 1057 or CAS[5] regime). The 728 regime offers open-ended contract duration and applies to a smaller number of staff members. The number of positions under 728 is capped, meaning that recruitments can only occur when an existing position becomes vacant. On the other hand, the CAS regime offers six-month contracts with fewer employment benefits, such as insurance or pensions, than the 728 regime. Temporary contracts under the CAS regime can be renewed without limits and are becoming the main way to hire new staff, extending beyond their intended temporary use across all Peruvian public entities. In the long run, this can reduce Osinergmin's attractiveness compared to the private sector

In 2013, the Peruvian government launched an employment public sector reform to be gradually implemented and overseen under the National Civil Service Authority (SERVIR). This reform is based on the provisions of Law No. 30057 (SERVIR law) that aims at implementing a single labour regime for public entities.

This would replace the 728 and CAS regimes currently in place and apply to all employees. Migration to the new regime is optional for existing staff, but staff under Law 728 would need to re-apply for their job to migrate. If they are not successful, they remain in their old post, under the old regime. CAS staff members will be required to transition to the new regime as CAS regime will cease to exist. To date, 412 have started the process to implement SERVIR law, but no public entity has fully migrated.

The 2016 OECD Public Governance Review of Peru, conducted as part of the OECD Country Programme for Peru, assessed, amongst other topics, the management of Peru's professional civil service and public administration reform agenda through the SERVIR law (see Box 2.3).

Box 2.3. Findings of the OECD Public Governance Review of Peru (2016) on building a stable and professional civil service in Peru

Peru's civil servants are currently under multiple labour regimes and complex employment regulations. This translates into a public labour system highly difficult to manage. For example, over 2000 government agencies established over 500 public employment regulations and over 400 different wage criteria.

In 2013, the Peruvian government issued the new Civil Service Law (30057) for implementing an ambitious civil service reform. The law has an implementation horizon of six years and SERVIR is charged with overseeing this implementation.

The purpose of the Civil Service Law is to establish a single and exclusive scheme for civil servants at national, regional and local levels. A new pay system will be implemented for those in the new regime, with the intent to improve transparency and equity across public entities. In addition, it articulates a strategic policy rationale for the civil service reform, emphasising merit and professionalism.

The new Civil Service Law was designed based on best practice across OECD countries, and, once implemented, is expected to create a lasting impact by significantly improving the organisation, capacity, professionalism and stability of the civil service.

Nonetheless, the transition to the new regime will likely take much longer as the transition is not automatic. Civil servants can choose between transitioning to the new regime and remaining in their previous regime. Furthermore, existing civil servants will need to apply to posts in the new regime and go through a competitive process to be appointed. If they are not successful, they remain in their old post, under the old regime. It should be noted that all temporary staff (CAS) will be required to transition to the new regime.

Source: (OECD, 2016[2]), *OECD Public Governance Reviews: Peru: Integrated Governance for Inclusive Growth*, OECD Public Governance Reviews, https://dx.doi.org/10.1787/9789264265172-en.

Recruitment

The selection process for staff is publicly advertised and handled by a Recruitment Committee with full autonomy to render their decision. The process is competency-based on a set of criteria (i.e. education, skills, experience) for each position (i.e. candidate profile). Each specific criterion has a score and the successful candidate is the person who achieves the highest score. Results are published on Osinergmin's website.

The selection process is carried out by the Committee who represents the areas where the positions are located, the general management and the Human Resource Management (HRM). When the internal invitation finishes without result, then a process open to the public is broadcast through different means (web page, Facebook, newspaper notices). For each invitation, the characteristics and requirements of the position are assessed. This consists of several stages: review of the resume, knowledge test and interview with the applicant.

In some special circumstances designated by the Board of Directors, different recruitment processes apply, for example, members of the Administrative Tribunal of Energy and Mines Sanctions (TASTEM) and Appeals Board of User Claims (JARU) who are selected by the Board of Directors. Members of the Tribunal for the Solution of Controversies are selected by the PCM. Recruitment is competitive for Osinergmin. Recruitment processes normally attract more than one hundred applicants, especially for junior positions which are comparative in nature to the private sector in terms of remuneration.

Post-employment restrictions are governed by Law 27588, which establishes prohibitions for civil servants such as Board members, senior officials, advisors and members of administrative tribunals, as well as officers or public servants that have had access to privileged information or whose opinion has been determinant in decision-making, are subject to a one-year post-employment restriction. This includes providing services under contractual arrangement, accepting remuneration, being part of the Board of Directors, directly or indirectly acquiring shares of a company associated with the sector, signing contracts with companies, or participating in employment with companies.

Staff members subject to post-employment restrictions have to sign a legal document committing not to violate the terms and conditions of the policy. There has been no instance of a supervision of the application of these provisions. Osinergmin has stated that these provisions do cause some difficulty recruiting new personnel.

To avoid conflict of interest, any person who owns more than 1% of shares of a company related to the competency of the regulator cannot be appointed as a member of the board or hired as a director, legal representative, entity, employee or consultant of a regulatory agency.

Senior management recruitment

The President of the Board is appointed for a five-year term by the Presidency of the Council of Ministers. The General Manager is appointed by the President of the Board of Directors, taking into account the profile and requirements for the position. The General Manager reports directly to the President of the Board. Some senior management positions are appointed by the President of the Board without term limits as "*puestos de confianza*" or "trusted positions". These positions include the General Manager, Administration and Finance Manager, Corporate Communications and Legal Advisor. These trusted positions can be dismissed by the President at any period in time. The new SERVIR labour regime limits *puestos de confianza* to 5% of total staff. While SERVIR is not fully implemented, Supreme Decree 084-2016-PCM establishes that the 5% rule is in full effect until the implementation of SERVIR. Osinergmin currently only has 2.7% of staff as *puestos de confianza.*

The other managers are recruited through a public selection process which ensures the hiring of personnel according to professional or technical merit. For this purpose, there are established internal procedures and mechanisms regarding the means and systems for issuing a call for applications, recruiting, evaluating and selecting candidates.

The members of the Board of Directors are appointed to staggering terms, described in more detail in Box 2.4.

The transition to the new SERVIR labour regime also modifies the regulations governing senior management. For example, senior managers will need to go through the formal recruitment process and all dismissals shall require proper justification, such as failing to accomplish individual goals. Term limits will also be introduced for all senior managers, which will be for three years and can be renewed for another two terms. After three terms, the official must leave the organisation.

Remuneration

Staff members of Osinergmin are remunerated according to limits ascribed by Supreme Decree and endorsed by the Chairman of the Council of Ministers and the Minister of Economy and Finances.[6] The current salaries were established in 2006 and are not indexed to inflation (see Table 2.10).

At the more junior level, the regulator believes these salaries are competitive with private industry. As result of this, between 20% and 30% of public merit contests to fill the positions are occupied by staff members who are already working at Osinergmin, as they believe that there is a career line within the entity.

However, recruiting and retaining senior managers is more difficult, mainly because their salary scales are not competitive vis-à-vis industry. In partial response, the government issued Supreme Decree No. 024-2018-EF in 2018, raising the President of the Board of Directors salary to PEN 28 000 (USD 7 692, approximately) to be more competitive with industry.

Table 2.10. Remuneration scales at regulatory agencies in Peru (in PEN)

Job category	Minimum monthly salary	Maximum monthly salary
President	28 000	28 000
General Manager	15 600	15 600
Director, associate director or advisor	14 000	15 600
Professional I	10 700	14 900
Professional II	7 000	11 500
Professional III	5 100	10 400
Analyst	3 400	5 700
Assistant	1 900	2 500

Note: By Supreme Decree No. 172-2013-EF of 15 July 2013.
Source: Information provided by Osinergmin, 2018.

As stated above (Box 2.3), the SERVIR reform aims at gradually achieving a consolidated single employment framework, harmonising not only the employment terms, but also the remuneration of civil servants. Osinergmin has not fully migrated to the regime but has been implementing some of the law's provisions. Migration to the civil service regime may further reduce Osinergmin's competitiveness to attract and maintain qualified professionals, exacerbated by the post-employment restrictions in place.

Talent recruitment, retention and training

Osinergmin offers a full compensation package to attract and retain staff, based on three essential elements:

- Benefits: 100% health care coverage for staff employed under the 728 regime, including for their beneficiaries that is defined as children and parents. This can be maintained at a low cost when retiring from the organisation. Also includes life insurance offered immediately upon employment. All staff have access to low-cost catering at the office and well-being programmes that can be also used by family members, flexible summer hours, and a free day for birthdays. They also strike deals for corporate discounts for items such as cinema, gyms, education centres, medical centre, etc.
- Growth: Osinergmin offers training programmes and a corporate university programme to help employees gain the tools and skills to improve their performance in line with institutional objectives (*Plan de Capacitación de Osinergmin*). This also includes links with foreign training organisations and international co-operation to promote high-quality training in other countries on issues related to the sector. Internal recognition is given to teams who achieve strategic cross-cutting objectives.
- Team building: Osinergmin is developing a project of cultural alignment to promote behaviours that enhance the achievement of strategic objectives. The project will be mandatory for employees to participate. Osinergmin also promotes team building through celebration of important special dates, such as Christmas or summer courses, which includes families.

Osinergmin has further focused on increasing employees professional capacities using training and strategic partnerships.

For more 16 years, Osinergmin has been operating a national programme aimed at recruiting young graduates from engineering, economics and law. Called the University Extension Course, the admission test attracts over 2 500 applicants, 90 of which are admitted. After two months of training, the top 30 are selected to do an internship at Osinergmin until the end of the year. They can then apply to vacancies or provide supervision services for the regulator.

Osinergmin is the first public entity to have its Human Resources Internship certified by the Good Employers Association, contributing to its brand as an employer. In addition, an annual event to which all staff are invited provides a forum to reward good performance publicly.

Osinergmin's staff turnover rate has been stable around 16% between 2015 and 2017. Moreover, according to the bi-annual "Great Places to Work Survey", staff satisfaction reached a 10-year high in 2017 with a 75% satisfaction rate.

Performance assessment and training

The performance of staff is managed through an online system allows staff to enter their individual goals programmed every quarter. The goals have been previously agreed between the managers and the staff. This system also enables entering the indicator on which the fulfilment of each goal is assessed. Each of Osinergmin's officers and staff conducts a quarterly evaluation of their goals in the System.

Each of the management instruments has its own set of specific indicators, whose purpose is to measure the progress of Osinergmin in their implementation. Each instrument also has its own control cycle, the most far-reaching being the Indicator-Based Management

Model and the Management Report, which are announced to all personnel and the Board respectively.

Osinergmin has a staff training committee made up of HRM staff and elected staff members nominated through an open invitation to al staff. This Commission defines the general guidelines of the training that is carried out each year, which is distributed and published through the intranet of the Institution.

Code of ethics

Osinergmin does not have an institutional code of conduct, but rather is governed by the Civil Service Ethics Code (Law 27815) that establishes ethical principles for civil servants. These regulations govern relations between Osinergmin staff and the regulated sector. Osinergmin also obtained certification ISO 37001:2016, which specifies requirements and provides guidance for establishing and improving an anti-bribery management system.

When new staff are hired, they should follow an induction course where they learn, amongst other topics, the definition of Osinergmin`s values (commitment, excellency, service, integrity and autonomy) and the Civil Service Ethics Code. The process for any fault, including those established in the Law of the Code of Ethics of the public function, is governed by the Civil Service Law and its regulations. This has been included in the Internal Regulation of Civil Servants (*Reglamento Interno de los Servidores Civiles*) of Osinergmin.

Article 8 of the Civil Service Ethics Code sets public servants ethical prohibitions. One of these prohibitions is to maintain relationships or accept situations, in which context, personal, business, economic or financial interests might conflict with the fulfilment of the duties and functions performed by the employee. Another prohibition for staff members is to obtain or to try benefits or illegal advantages, for himself or others, by means of the use of its charge or influences. Likewise, the General Regulations of Osinergmin provide that Board members should disclose potential conflict of interests and ultimately abstain from participating in decisions related to the conflict.

With respect to disciplinary administrative procedures, sanctions are proposed by the Human Resources Manager and approved by the President of the Board. Any appeals are resolved by the Civil Service Court managed by SERVIR. If a manager is declared responsible for a crime, Osinergmin terminates the labour contract.

Process

As stated above, Osinergmin was created in the late-1990s towards the end of the macroeconomic and structural reforms era. Its organisational structure and processes reflect both the original efforts to establish autonomous regulators in key economic sectors, as well as the evolution of the regulator over time in a political environment that added new roles and responsibilities.

Osinergmin is headed by a Board of Directors and President of the Board who set the strategic direction of the regulator. Its General Management conducts the technical functions in regards to tariff regulation, energy supervision, and mining supervision. This is supported by horizontal functions carried out by various departments, including support and analytical functions.

The regulator supports the use of regulatory quality tools, such as RIA, stakeholder engagement and *ex post* evaluation, to varying degrees to improve the decision-making process.

Decision making and governance structure

The Board of Directors is the highest authority in the regulatory agency and members are appointed by the Executive. It is a non-executive body composed of six members appointed to five-year terms by a commission designated by the central government and can be re-appointed for one additional term (see Box 2.4).

In the event of a Board member leaving before the end of their term, the new member is only appointed for the remaining amount of time. Vacancies must be filled within 30 days of the expiration of a member's term.

To maintain the independence of the Board, the only interaction between the Board and staff of the regulator is through sessions of the Board and with respect to the issues being addressed in those sessions. The decision making process is as follows:

- The Board adopts its decisions in the sessions, for which an Agenda is proposed.
- The divisions of the General Management are responsible for proposing and sustaining specific sectoral issues entered into the agenda of the session of the Board, which must have the approval of the General Manager.
- The topics and their support proposed in the agenda are made available to the members of the Board with at least two days prior to the date of the session.
- During the session, if necessary, those responsible for the proposed topic briefly explain the content of the proposal and answer the questions of the members of the Governing Council.

As of October 2018, the composition of the Board was two lawyers, two engineers, and one economist. One position was vacant at the time of writing. Osinergmin believes this diversity is important so that its decisions can be taken evaluating economic, legal and technical aspects of the corresponding sector. However, there have been no women on the Board in the last ten years. Historically, there have also been a number of Board members resignations (Table 2.11), which shortened the effective duration of some members' mandates. This can disrupt continuity and limit the Board's ability to provide sound advice.

The Board is responsible for the administration and supervision of contracts and other generic processes; overseeing the stakeholder engagement process; and setting a clear process for executing the mandate of the organisation. The Board exerts both normative and regulatory functions via resolutions, and issues non-binding technical opinions on concession contracts organised by the Government. The Board also appoints and removes members of the Collegiate Bodies, as well as a sanction function in the second instance.

Table 2.11. 10-year history of Osinergmin board members

Member	Role	Start date	End date
Daniel Schmerler Vainstein	President	2017	2022
Antonio Miguel Angulo Zambrano	Board member	2017	2021
Fénix Noé Suto Fujita	Board Member	2015	2020
César Antonio Sánchez Módena	Board member	2015	2019
Richard Alberto Navarro Rodríguez	Board member	2017	2018[1]
Carlos Federico Barreda Tamayo	Board member	2013	2018[2]
Jesús Tamayo Pacheco	President	2012	2017
José Ignacio Távara Martín	Board member	2013	2015[3]
Pedro Félix Remy Álvarez Calderón	Board member	2010	2012[4]
David Alfredo Tuesta Cárdenas	Board member	2007	2012
Pablo Berckholtz Salinas	Board member	2008	2012[5]
Alfredo Dammert Lira	President	2007	2012

Notes: 1. finished his term in August 2018 and PCM's appointment of a new member is pending at the time of writing. 2. received an extension according to Supreme Decree No. 082-2018-PCM. 3, 4, 5 resigned.
Source: Information provided by Osinergmin, 2018.

Box 2.4. Board of Directors selection process

Criteria for selection as a Board member are:

- Be a professional with no less than ten (10) years of practice;
- Have recognised professional solvency and suitability, by way of no less than three years of experience in a position of executive management, with understanding of the decision making in public or private companies; or five years of experience in matters related to the competence of the regulatory body; and,
- Having completed studies at the Master's level in subjects related to the competence of the regulatory body.

All members of the Board are selected by:

- Review of candidates by a selection committee composed of one member proposed by the PCM, one member proposed by Indecopi, one member proposed by MEF and one member proposed by the sectorial ministry related to regulator activities;
- The President of the Council of Ministers submits to the President of the Republic the final list of selected candidates; and
- The President of the Republic appoints the member of the Board by Supreme Resolution, which will be endorsed by the President of the Council of Ministers, the Minister of Economy and Finance and the sectorial ministry related to the regulator activities.

Board Members can be dismissed due to legal impediments supervening the appointment, unjustified absences from two consecutive sessions unless authorised, or in the case of serious misconduct. The same one-year restriction on post-employment for employees of the regulator applies to board members.

Source: Law No. 27332; Supreme Decree 103-2012-PCM; Supreme Decree No. 014-2008-PCM; (OECD, 2016[1]), *Regulatory Policy in Peru: Assembling the Framework for Regulatory Quality*, OECD Reviews of Regulatory Reform, http://dx.doi.org/10.1787/9789264260054-en.

Board members are remunerated PEN 3 000 (approximately USD 900) per month, with the requirement to attend two meetings each month. However, the President or a majority of Board members can request to meet more times. Regulations forbid Osinergmin to pay Board members for additional sessions. The President is the only member with a monthly remuneration. Changes to these limits require amendment to regulations issued by the Executive.

Votes are determined by a simple majority of the members attending. The agenda and minutes of Board meetings are posted on the Osinergmin website.

Information to support Board meetings are usually sent a few days before the meeting. The technical staff of the regulator compiles a "supporting report" for the Board, which includes an analysis of the market, problem, and a proposal of options and a resolution. Technical teams are invited to Board meetings to present their analysis.

President of the Board of Directors

The President of the Board of Directors performs the regulator executive functions. The President is responsible for setting the strategic direction and functions of the Board; exerts executive and administrative functions; and reports on behalf of the regulator to the PCM and MEF.

The President is selected through public contest. A Selection Committee composed of two members from the PCM, one member proposed by MEF and one by the MEM proposes a list of applicants to the President of the Council of Ministers, who submits to the President of the Republic the proposed selected candidate. The President of the Board of Directors is then appointed via a Supreme Decree

The President presides over the Board, implement the decisions of the Board, and represent Osinergmin before public authorities and at national or foreign institutions. As stated above, the President also appoints or removes the General Manager and approves, at the proposal of the General Manager, the hiring of line managers and management level officials, as well as their promotion, suspension and removal. Finally, the President approves the institutional budget, balance sheets and financial statements as well as the Institutional Management Plan and administrative policies.

General Manager

The General Manager is responsible for the legal and administrative responsibilities of Osinergmin. Appointed by the President, the General Manager plans, organises, manages, executes and supervises the administrative, operational, economic and financial activities of Osinergmin.

The General Manager also attends sessions of the Board, but does not have a voting function. For discussions pertaining to appeals of decisions made by the General Management, the General Manager must withdraw from the session.

According to Osinergmin's Organisation and Functions manual (*Manual de Organización y Funciones-MOF*), both the President of the Board and the General Manager can hire technical advisors. The other members of the Board have no supporting staff and their internal information requests can take a long time before they are processed. At the time of writing, the President of the Board of Directors has five advisors, and the General Manager has four.

Organisational structure

Osinergmin is organised into five sections (see Figure 2.3 for full organigram):

- **Strategic bodies:** Board of Directors, President of the Board and the General Manager, described above.
- **Line bodies:** Responsible for developing regulations and conducting supervisions according to their specific duties.
- **Advisory bodies:** Responsible for developing and proposing advice and initiatives to the General Manager on issues related to Legal Advice, Planning, Budget and Modernisation, and Policy and Economic Analysis.
- **Support bodies:** Provide the General Management with human and financial resource management, IT services, and communications and international relations.
- **Dispute resolution bodies:** Responsible for handling complaints and appeals to the decisions of the regulator, and is supported by a technical secretariat.

Figure 2.3. Osinergmin's organisational structure

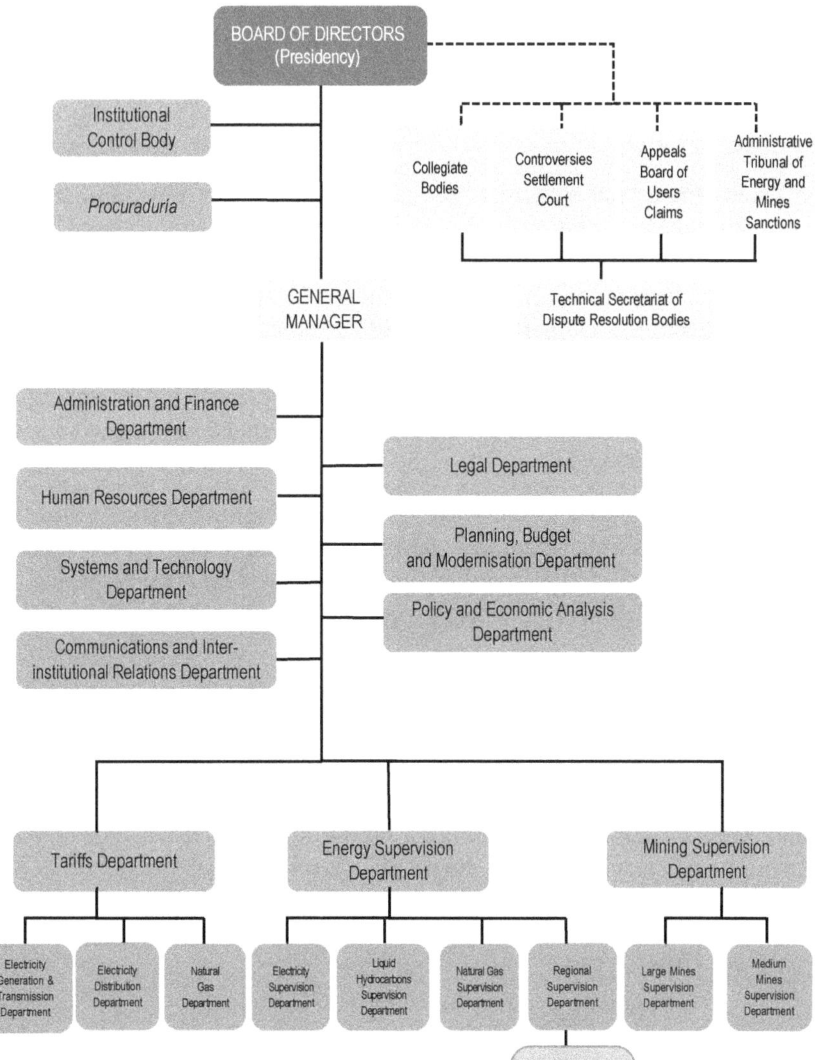

Seven departments are directly accountable to the General Manager. In addition, the Regional Offices Department reports both to the Energy Supervision Department and the GM.

The Finance and Administration Department manages resources and collects the contributions from the industry. It is also charged with procurement, accounting, document management, this department produces the financial statements that are sent to MEF and verified by the *Contraloria de la Republica.*

The Human Resources Department manages staff recruitment, training, procurement of external intellectual services and monitors compliance with labour conditions and standards. The Systems and Technology Department is in charge of all matters related to IT, platforms and digitalisation.

The Communications and Inter-institutional Relations Department handles all media requests and the relationship with the national press, engages in outreach activities with companies, public bodies and citizens, produces the annual report and is in charge of all the internal communication.

The Department aims to increase Osinergmin's visibility and recognition in line with the PEI's objectives. For instance, they engaged in media campaigns through press releases, interviews and press conferences in order to advertise the new LPG requirements among consumers. These requirements meant that each LPG gas filling plant has to place a label with the exact information of gas cylinders. Eighteen months after the introduction of the regulation, compliance was high and 66% of plants placed labels on their gas cylinders.

The Legal Department ensures that all of Osinergmin's norms and actions are in accordance with the law and provides guidelines on horizontal issues affecting all technical departments. In addition, specialised lawyers are present across all those departments. In the absence of a nominated *Procurador*, the work of the Department also stretches to representing Osinergmin in public court cases (although litigation is contracted out and supervised by the Department). The Department also engages with legislators and government officials by issuing proposals for changing laws and procedures. For instance, Osinergmin recently proposed that judicial review cases should be limited to assessing the legality and not the merit of Osinergmin's decisions.

The Planning and Budgeting Department has wide-ranging responsibilities related to long-term plans, operational planning, and annual budgeting. The Department also supervises processes such as the Quality Management System (QMS), health and safety, information security, the service charter and the adherence to international quality standards (ISO).

The Policy and Economic Analysis Department (GPAE), performs a mix of internal and external functions. Internally, amongst other functions, the GPAE participate to the budgeting and planning processes; promote the development and adoption of regulatory quality tools such as RIA; and support the Board in developing internal recommendations and guidelines. Externally, GPAE monitors key policy and market developments in the energy and mining sectors, produces Sectoral Economic Reports (*Reportes de Análisis Económico Sectorial*) and working papers on regulatory policy issues. It is also in charge of designing, distributing and analysing the responses to the questionnaire measuring Osinergmin's reputation (EPERS).

The role of the Tariff Departments, the Energy Supervision Department and the Mining Supervision Department are detailed in the section on Roles and objectives. The structure of these Departments is largely a legacy of the building blocks that have composed the regulator over time. Some co-operation across Departments takes place thanks to the good personal relationship between staff members, but official co-ordination meetings on technical matters are not part of the weekly routine and most Departments have sufficient in-house expertise.

User protection

In addition to regulatory and supervision functions, Osinergmin facilitate consumer protection in the energy sector by allowing users to complain via the administrative courts about the quality of service and access in the sector. This can be accomplished by visiting one of the 25 regional offices and 15 decentralised offices across Peru, by telephone through a Call Centre open during business hours, or online by filling in a form on the regulator's web portal.

The Communications and Inter-Institutional Relations Department develops campaigns to empower consumers, such as educational programmes for students, as well as for disabled and blind consumers. In addition, Osinergmin has developed mobile applications to help users with the support they need. These include:

- *Facilito Electricidad*: Enables the user to report problems to the electricity company that provides the service. The information reported is sent to the electricity company to solve the problem, and Osinergmin supervise compliance of the service.
- *Facilito Combustible:* Enables users to find fuel service stations near their location and compare prices.
- *Tukuy Rikuy:* Meaning "Who sees and hears everything" in the local Quechuan language, this SMS-based service implemented nationwide allows users to submit complaints and requests for service for energy on any mobile device, regardless of the technology. Messages arrive in real time to the electricity company in the area and to Osinergmin. This allows for immediate action, eliminating barriers to access, mobilisation costs, and time.

Most complaints and claims are made in writing and personally at Osinergmin's offices. Osinergmin is noticing that since the implementation of the mobile applications and the "*Tukuy Rikuy*" system, the number of complaints through technological means has increased.

Regulatory quality

In 2016, the PCM issued Law Decree No. 1310 on Regulatory Quality Assessment (RQA), with draft rulings and guidelines in July 2017. The full rulings and guidelines are expected in 2018. The RQA is a procedure to assess regulations that establish administrative procedures to identify, reduce and/or eliminate unnecessary, unjustified, disproportionate, or redundant procedures (Ministerial Resolution No. 196-PCM-2017). The rulings and guidelines apply to all public entities of the Executive branch.

The Decree and support documents require all government entities to perform RQAs on all regulations that establish administrative procedures. The Decree establishes three actions: requiring an *ex ante* assessment of impacts for new procedures, a review of the regulatory stock, and a revision to the regulatory stock every three years to reduce burdens. The decree limits this to procedural changes related to administrative processes and not for all regulatory measures.

A Multi-Sectoral Commission on Regulatory Quality (MCRQ) was also establish as a permanent body that reports to the Presidency of the Council of Ministers. The MCRQ serves to assess and validate the RQAs conducted by public entities of the executive branch according to four principles: legality, necessity, effectiveness, and proportionality. The MCRQ issues its observations and proposals for improving the measure, which is sent to the public entity for correction or acceptance and then back to the MCRQ for validation. The MCRQ can also propose the dismissal of an administrative procedure if it does not meet the principles of legality or necessity.

Independently and in parallel to the development of the PCM RQA, three regulators – Osinergmin, OSIPTEL and OSITRAN – developed manuals and guidelines for assessing the impacts of regulatory decisions. These manuals extend the scope of analysis and application of assessments to include a wider scope of regulatory decisions, and not just those affecting administrative procedures. Osinergmin rolled out their own RIA process in co-operation with the OECD in 2017. The regulator also uses stakeholder engagement and, to a lesser degree, some *ex post* evaluation to improve the quality of regulatory decisions.

Regulatory impact assessments

As of October 2018, one full RIA was completed,[7] a second RIA is underway, 16 mini-RIAs have been completed and a further 18 are underway (as of the end of 2017). Mini-RIAs are an abridged version of the full RIAs, which are intended for the institution to learn the process and the analysis that goes into the *ex ante* evaluations. Table 2.12 explains the difference instances where a full or mini-RIA is required.

Table 2.12. Methodological differences between Osinergmin's full and mini-RIA

Processes	Full RIA	Mini RIA
Pre-consultation with stakeholders regarding the problem	Required	No
Definition of problem	Required	Required
Definition of objectives	Required	Required
Policy options	Required	Required
Costs and benefits of each policy option	Quantitative	Qualitative
Comparison of options	Required	Required
Mechanisms of implementation, compliance and monitoring	Required	Partial
Public consultation with stakeholders	Required	Optional

Source: Information provided by Osinergmin, 2018.

The main differences are that the full RIA includes a quantification of the costs and benefits, whereas in a mini RIA these are described qualitatively. The full RIA also requires more rigorous analysis of the mechanisms of implementation, compliance and monitoring as well as a public stakeholder consultation.

Guidance for full RIAs are contained in the Guidance on Regulatory Policy No. 1 and in various memoranda published by the regulator. In addition to these publications, Osinergmin has hosted workshops on the RIA process conducted by the OECD as well as by its own staff familiar with the methodology.

The departments proposing the regulation are the ones responsible for initiating and preparing the RIAs with extensive support and guidance from the Policy and Economic Analysis department and legal specialists within Osinergmin.

RIAs are submitted to the Board, which can return the RIA to the relevant department and resubmit after the comments from the Board have been addressed.

Methodologies for the calculation of costs and benefits have been implemented since 2001 (article 7 of Supreme Decree No. 054-2001-PCM).

The GPAE and Legal departments review and formally approve the assessments to ensure quality, provide comments, and provide support to the relevant departments responsible for the assessments before they go to the Board. If either department has comments, the RIA is returned to the line manager to incorporate recommendations. The revised RIAs are then sent to the Board for their review, in accordance with the guidelines.

Stakeholder engagement

Public consultations are not mandatory in Peru. The only form of consultation required by law is to publish new laws and regulations in the Official Gazette, web page or other instrument at least 30 days before its entry into force to receive comments and make necessary modifications.

According to the *Regulatory Policy Review of Peru* (OECD, 2016[1]), all economic regulators do prepare a matrix of comments that assembles stakeholders' comments on regulatory proposals with an evaluation from the regulator regarding whether and how the comment will be considered.

Osinergmin's stakeholder engagement process includes the publication of all the information of the process, the pre-publication of the tariff-fixing resolution and the support of the decisions adopted by the regulatory agency in the public consultations. Most of these efforts are conducted via the regulator's website, with public consultations used when necessary (normally in regards to important issues). The RIA, where applicable, is also published with the draft proposal for comments.

Stakeholders do not submit comments on *ex post* evaluations but, in certain cases, may provide input into the impact evaluation process. For FOSE, internal stakeholders, specifically Osinergmin's Board and the tariff regulation department that administers the subsidy, comment on the report. For FISE evaluation being conducted this year,

Osinergmin is considering using surveys and interviews with beneficiaries and focus groups. Additionally, a large quantity of data is collected on LPG distribution and beneficiaries of the LPG subsidy. Though data analysis and monitoring that is part of the LPG program, FISE is able to identify potential problems and improve the design of the programme.

Furthermore, the LMOR requires regulators to have one or more User Councils for stakeholder participation, However, Osinergmin's Users Council does not engage on practices on consultation (see Box 2.5).

Box 2.5. User Councils

According to the LMOR, economic regulators are also required to have one or more User Councils for stakeholder participation on each sector. Council members are appointed by the Board for a two-year period. These councils can be local, regional or national depending on the characteristics of the markets. Regulators publish a call for potential candidates to the council, as well as a provisional list of candidates and a final list of elected members. Member councils come from consumer associations, universities, professional colleges, non-profit organisations and business organisations not related with the regulated entities. The LMOR provides that the positions on the Councils are unpaid. However, it also states that the regulators must finance their activities.

The financial resources assigned to the Council's functioning should be included in the institutional budget of the regulators. Board of Directors Resolution No. 152-2015-OS/CD (Resolución de Consejo Directivo 152-2015-OS/CD), states that Osinergmin has one national Users Council comprising five members. Three members are selected from a list of candidates proposed by consumers and users associations. Two members are from a list of candidates proposed by energy and hydrocarbons professional bodies, universities that offer professional careers related to energy, natural gas or hydrocarbons, non-profit organisations related to the same sectors, and by business organisations not related to the regulated entities. The members are elected for a two-year period and do not receive a salary.

For the 2017-19 period, the Users Council comprises one member of each of the following institutions:

- *Caudal* (institute of consumer protection).
- *Equidad* (centre of citizen protection).
- *Asociación San Francisco* (association for the defence of consumers rights).
- *Asociación de Pequeños y Medianos Industriales del Perú- Región Piura* (association of small and medium industrial businesses of Peru, Piura region).
- *Colegio de Economistas de Piura* (professional body of economists of Piura).

Despite this requirement, Osinergmin does not consult with the Users Council on proposed initiatives. There are no legal consequences of not having well-functioning Users Councils.

Source: Information provided by Osinergmin and complemented by an analysis of current regulations.

Ex post *reviews*

In accordance with the PCM RQA, economic regulators in Peru are only required to undertake stock reviews and *ex post* evaluations for regulations that add administrative procedures. Osinergmin does voluntarily undertake some *ex post* evaluation on its funds and some regulations that are not covered by the PCM RQA. The GPAE department is responsible for all evaluations. The methodologies were developed for each case and noted below, though FISE methodology was an MEF guide on results-based evaluation.

In 2017, Osinergmin reviewed the stock of procedures according to RQA initiative of the PCM and presented it on 29 September of 2017. Since that date each new procedure has its RQA evaluation.

Osinergmin's Electric Social Compensation Fund (FOSE) is a cross-subsidy programme on the tariffs paid by consumers who consume less than 100kWh per month and targets low-income households. An annual evaluation is conducted to see whether the program correctly targets the population. The analysis is quantitative and includes a calculation of inclusion and exclusion errors (percentage) as well as the distribution of subsidies by income level. This is subsequently compared to the previous years' data. If the errors are found to be increasing, Osinergmin looks for ways to improve the targeting of the subsidy.

FOSE evaluation is conducted annually after the results of the General Household Survey conducted by Osinergmin become available.

FISE has several different programmes associated with it. In 2015/16, it was subjected to an intermediate evaluation by the OECD in collaboration with Osinergmin to evaluate the impact of the LPG subsidy.

In 2018, FISE will undergo two additional impact evaluations. The first will evaluate the LPG subsidy to provide targeted cross-subsidies for the use of LPG. It will focus on health indicators and the extent to which the program successfully encouraged switching among low-income households from biomass to LPG. The second is an intermediate impact evaluation that will look at the residential natural gas installation program, which provides partial or full financing for connecting homes to the natural gas network. This intermediate impact evaluation will measure impact in terms of savings to the consumer and the quantity of gas used. A guide was produced on how to focus subsidies and the relevant indicators.

Seven impact evaluations have also been conducted on regulatory policies. These were *ad hoc*, so the criteria varied for each evaluation but focused on social and economic dimensions. These impact evaluations are:

- Supervision of street lighting: evaluated the cost-benefit ratio of the change in the supervision process using consumer's willingness to pay.
- Energy losses evaluation: evaluated the impact of a regulatory change aimed at reducing energy losses by measuring savings to consumers
- Safety and accident prevention: evaluated the impact of a change in supervision practices in terms of deaths avoided.
- Metrological control: evaluated the impact of a change in metrological control supervision in terms of social costs and benefits.

- Supervision of mining activities: evaluated the impact of a change in supervision practices in terms of deaths avoided.
- Supervision of electricity meters: measured the impact of supervision practices in savings to consumers.
- Supervision of gasoline and diesel quality: evaluated the impact of a reduction in the number of low quality gas stations in terms benefits to consumers.

Regional offices

Osinergmin operates 25 regional offices in charge of supervising services provided to customers in the downstream part of the electricity, gas and hydrocarbon sectors. They employ 170 staff members nation-wide, including seven people in each regional office and six in the Lima headquarters. Most of the growth in the regulator's staff has taken place in the regional offices in recent years and a large share of the budget (more than 20% in 2016) is allocated to these offices.

The main line of action for these offices is to empower consumers by receiving complaints either in person or through their call centre. They also receive and process the SMS complaints received through the *Tukuy Rikuy* system. Where necessary, complaints are then forwarded to the Lima office.

The Regional Offices also support local efforts to ensure the consistency and security of services and infrastructure with the regulated entities, particularly where power outages are frequent. For gas, they focus on the security of the service as well as expanding the system. They also co-ordinate the transportation of hydrocarbons through maintaining a list of registered carriers that are validated at the national level.

Finally, the offices work to identify gaps in the legal framework that require a fix from Osinergmin headquarters or MEM.

To promote co-ordination, they work closely with the Lima headquarters as well as both regulated entities and consumers. With regulated entities, they meet with electricity companies to identify areas where investment is most needed, especially in areas where companies are state owned. With consumers, they run regional assemblies that offer another pathway to offer complaints and work to understand issues to inform supervisions and foster a preventative approach with companies.

Enforcement and inspections

Osinergmin is charged with supervising the safety of infrastructure in the energy and mining sectors. Supervision powers include the ability to inspect operators and infrastructure managers, and impose sanctions on regulated entities. Starting with a supervision report, which identifies evidence of non-compliance, the sanctioning process continues with the communication and levying of a fine onto the regulated entity. The procedure needs to be approved by the General Manager of Osinergmin. The Administrative Court of Appeals for Sanctions on Energy and Mining Issues (TASTEM) serves as the appeals body in the second instance. After the second instance decision, the regulated entity can file a judicial review. Table 2.13 summarises the cumulative amount of sanctions levied on all sectors since Osinergmin began its work.

Due to Osinergmin's change of mandate (see Role and Objectives section above), inspection functions are no longer related to the supervision of environmental and labour issues. OEFA and SUNAFIL are the Peruvian agencies that conduct inspections on these issues respectively. In addition, MEM, and other regional and national authorities can carry out inspections mainly on environmental issues.

There are circumstances in which inspectors from the different agencies conduct their inspections at the same time as Osinergmin (i.e. oil spills, large mining accidents). Regulated companies perceive that the various agencies face overlapping requests or duplicated reports. Moreover, companies perceive that the complexity of technical standards and regulations makes difficult to comply with all requests.

Table 2.13. Administrative fines issued and pending, by stage from 1998-2017

Stage	Amount (PEN)
First instance	54 078 061.48
Reconsideration	13 911 926.49
Appeal	293 725 110.69
Complaint	14 590 711.29
Coercive	113 401 079.05
Judicial proceedings	343 233 652.60
TOTAL	**832 940 541.60**

Source: Information provided by Osinergmin, 2018.

The diverse agencies carry out *ad hoc* and informal co-ordination when inspecting the same sites. There is no evidence of formal and institutional co-ordination between agencies. On a case-by-case basis, entities such OEFA and Osinergmin share certain information about the common inspections. Each organisation then publishes web portal the results of inspections related to events with large social and environmental impact.

Osinergmin, OEFA and SUNAFIL recognise the importance of making their mandate clear for the energy and mining sectors. In that sense, these agencies and MEM issued a List of Technical Functions that defines the legal competences of Osinergmin, OEFA and SUNAFIL. However, there is no evidence of a joint supervision strategy.

Osinergmin also recognises the importance of fostering a safety culture. For example, the regulator has conducted impact evaluations of Osinergmin's supervisions in the number of deaths avoided. However, there is no evidence of an integrated strategy to improve prevention.

Appeals

Osinergmin has four administrative dispute resolution bodies (*órganos resolutivos*) governed by its internal regulations *(Reglamento de los órganos resolutivos de Osinergmin, Resolución de Consejo Directivo 044-2018*) see Table 2.14:

- Collegiate Bodies (*Cuerpos Colegiados de Solución de Controversias*).
- Controversies Settlement Court (*Tribunal de Solución de Controversias*).
- Appeal Board of Users Claims (*Junta de Apelaciones de Reclamos de Usuarios – JARU*).
- Administrative Tribunal of Energy and Mines Sanctions (TASTEM).

Table 2.14. Osinergmin's administrative dispute resolution bodies

Stage	Controversies between regulated entities	Consumer complaints	Sanctions
First instance	Collegiate Bodies	Launch complaint directly with the regulated entity	Line department responsible for enforcing the regulation.
Second Instance	Controversies Settlement Court	JARU	TASTEM

Source: Information provided by Osinergmin, 2018.

Cuerpos Colegiados de Solución de Controversias are first instance and non-permanent administrative bodies that resolve controversies between regulated companies. These may involve, for instance, controversies between transmission and distribution companies. When a dispute arises, the President appoints three members ad-hoc from an internal registry of candidates. However, the President can decide to appoint a permanent Cuerpo Colegiado.

Tribunal de Solución de Controversias resolves in second instance the appeals against the decisions issued by *Cuerpos Colegiados*. According to the LMOR, their members are appointed by Supreme Decree issued by the PCM. Since 2015, there have been delays in the PCM nominating the members of the Tribunal. This has resulted in the body not being able to meet given the lack of a legal number of members and, as a result, large delays have been accumulated. Businesses perceive this as being an issue with Osinergmin's efficiency rather than the result of delayed decisions by the Executive.

User complaints are filed to energy companies in first instance. The Osinergmin body JARU serves as the second instance. In some cases, JARU will also hear complaints of smaller regulated entities against the larger ones. The Board appoints the members of JARU for a three-year period.

Finally, TASTEM serves as the second instance administrative body for appealing sanctions in the energy and mining sector after companies have appealed to the Department that imposed those sanctions in the first instance. The Board also appoints their members for a three-year period.

Until 2008, the Board of Directors was ultimately responsible for adjudicating fines. Since the new TASTEM was created, appeals are addressed through this technical appellate body. The Board only retains ultimate responsibility for decisions on tariffs, including in the case of appeals by the companies.

A significant rise in the number of appeals is raising the toll of unresolved cases in all tribunals, including the JARU (1 522 unresolved cases in 2016 and 2 339 in 2017) and the TASTEM (407 unresolved cases in 2016 and 274 in 2017). Osinergmin is addressing this issue by hiring extra resources in 2018, leading to a 20% increase in personnel working across tribunals.

The second instance decisions (*Tribunal de Solución de Controversias*, JARU and TASTEM) can be appealed before administrative courts (*proceso contencioso administrativo*). Companies can also appeal Osinergmin's tariff setting decisions after asking for reconsideration of the Board of Directors.

Judicial reviews can be expensive and often take several years to complete. Users and regulated entities may use judicial review as a method to delay paying sanctions or being subjected to changes in tariffs. Regarding users, the payment of energy bills is suspended during a litigation process.

The Judiciary can decide the case both on the merit and on the process undertaken by Osinergmin. Most cases are decided in favour of Osinergmin. Nevertheless, the number of judicial reviews is rising (see Table 2.15).

Table 2.15. Osinergmin decisions appealed in courts and outcomes

Year	Number of decisions taken	Number of decisions appealed	Status (decision upheld, rejected, ongoing)
2018 (as of May)	5 329	181	Ongoing:179 Concluded: 2 Upheld:2 Rejected: 0
2017	13 472	520	Ongoing:507 Concluded: 13 Upheld:13 Rejected: 0
2016	12 189	378	Ongoing:324 Concluded: 54 Upheld: 53 Rejected: 1
2015	11 449	359	Ongoing:256 Concluded: 103 Upheld: 100 Rejected: 3
2014	10 980	471	Ongoing: 244 Concluded: 227 Upheld:220 Rejected:7

Source: Information provided by Osinergmin, 2018.

The number of appeals is rising both in the administrative dispute resolution bodies and the judiciary. Osinergmin is also considering the reason behind the growth in appeals. The following four areas have been identified, and deserve further analysis leading to remedial action by the responsible departments:

- Delays in nominating some of the TSC (*Tribunal por la resolución de controversias*) members by the PCM
- Complexity of the regulatory framework and a large number of new rules and norms issued each year leading to non-compliance
- A punitive supervision approach leading to a growing number of fines levied
- The increase in activities in more remote areas raising awareness about consumer rights and ways to complain

The *"procurador"* serves as the lawyer and public servant charged with the legal defence of public entities. This function is recognised in the Peruvian National Constitution (article 47) and in the State's Legal Defence System Law (*Ley del Sistema de Defensa Jurídica del Estado*). *Procuradores* are proposed and overseen by the Ministry of Justice. Osinergmin's *procurador* is currently a vacant position. In the interim, lawyers from the Legal Department exercise the defence of the entity.

Transparency and accountability

Transparency

Relations between Osinergmin staff and the regulated sector are governed by the Civil Service Ethics Code (Law 27815) that establishes ethical principles for civil servants. Based on these principles, Osinergmin employees are prohibited from obtaining personal or financial benefits from regulated industries.

All decisions made by Osinergmin are published on their website and, for regulatory decisions, in the Official Gazette *El Peruano*. Osinergmin also makes use of their website to publish the results from stakeholder engagements and information on sanctions, data, and outreach activities. Furthermore a variety of media, including social media, is used to communicate these outputs with the public. Osinergmin runs LinkedIn, Facebook, Twitter accounts and has developed an app available for both Android and iOS smartphones.

This is supported by the Communications and Inter-Institutional Relations Department (GCI), which has eight staff members supporting communications through social media, traditional media, and online. GCI also employs educational projects to inform users of their rights, programmes in schools to teach them how to prevent accidents, advertising campaigns, and facilitates co-ordination efforts with stakeholders and other government bodies. Their communication in inclusive, utilising methods to communicate with disabled persons as well as non-Spanish speaking communities, such as the Quechuan population.

Osinergmin has been proactive in adhering to international standards and gaining independent certification of their management processes. These certifications add to the credibility and transparency of institutional decisions and show Osinergmin's commitment to following international standards. The following systems have already been certified:

- Quality management systems (ISO 9001:2015)
- Environmental management systems (ISO 14001:2015)
- Occupation health and safety (OHSAS 18001:2008)
- Information security management (ISO 27001:2013)
- Anti-bribery management systems (ISO 37001:2016)
- Service Commitment Charter (UNE 93200)

The regulator is also in the process of obtaining an updated occupational health and safety certification.

Accountability to Congress

Osinergmin is accountable to Congress, while being overseen by the PCM and potentially called upon by MEM or other relevant government departments to provide information or opinions. Although Osinergmin publishes an annual report on their website, there is no requirement to officially share and present this with any State entities nor to present it before Congress. The PCM and MEF do require the regulator to report on certain indicators and meet reporting requirements; however, these are often fragmented.

However, it is common for the parliamentary commissions related to Osinergmin's work to invite the regulator annually to explain the results of its work, scope of jurisdiction, and actions to be carried out in the future. In the Congress of the Republic, there are two ordinary committees that study, monitor and carry out the political control of the Energy and Mines sector and the regulatory agency that has jurisdiction in said sector. These are the Energy and Mines Commission and the Consumer Defence Commission and Public Services Regulatory Agencies. Hearings usually take place in each Annual Session Period, as a new Executive Committee assumes the presidency of the commissions.

Regulatory authorities can also be called by the Plenary of Congress or the ordinary committees to report on issues under their jurisdiction that are being considered by the Congress, such as in the case of sector reforms.

In addition to the annual report on their results, both commissions invite Osinergmin to give a presentation on follow-up issues by the Executive Committee and/or members of the commission, which generally are related to a problem of regional or local nature. For instance, Table 2.16 outlines some of the main topics for which Osinergmin is summoned by the committees.

Table 2.16. Topics discussed by Osinergmin with the Ordinary Commissions of Congress

Committee	Topics
Energy and Mines Commission	• Application of electricity tariffs • Problems with some electricity companies • Quality of service in electric distribution systems • Non-conventional renewable energies • The problems with bottled LPG and wholesale LPG • Supervision and inspection of Osinergmin in the North Peruvian Pipeline • Global population access to natural gas and its relevance in the energy matrix • Investment plan in Lima for the expansion of the domestic natural gas network • Damages caused by third parties in the natural gas distribution system in Lima
Consumer Defense Commission	• Supervision and inspection of user service activities • Fuel sales prices and supervision • Osinergmin's functions in consumer protection and defence

Source: Information provided by Osinergmin, 2018.

Other ordinary commissions also invite Osinergmin, based on specific issues and situations that arise at the regional or local level to report and discuss on this topic. Among these commissions are the:

- Commission of Andean, Amazonian and Afro-Peruvian Peoples, Environment and Ecology;
- Commission for Decentralisation, Regionalisation, Local Governments and Modernisation of State Management;
- Labour and Social Security Commission.

The Congress can also initiate investigations on any matter of public interest, being mandatory to appear, by request, before the commissions in charge of said investigations. The commissions will promote an investigation procedure that guarantees the clarification of the facts and the formulation of conclusions and recommendations aimed at correcting standards and policies and/or sanctioning the behaviour of those responsible.

In the 2016-17 Annual Session Period, three investigation commissions were created related to sector issues and in which Osinergmin, according to its functions and jurisdiction, participated. These include:

- Special Multiparty Commission responsible for investigating and determining the responsibilities of officials and individuals and public and private institutions responsible for the oil spills in the North Peruvian Pipeline; whose purpose was to investigate and determine the causes and factors of business management, officials, individuals and public and private institutions that are liable for oil spills in the North Peruvian Pipeline, consequently determining liability for property damage, losses by the State, and also from the point of view of environmental damage, establishing environmental liabilities related to oil spills. For its investigation and report, the Investigating Commission sent Osinergmin six Requests for Information and invited it to a reserved session to answer the questions related to the actions that Osinergmin carried out, with respect to the operations of the North Peruvian Pipeline.
- Investigating Commission in charge of investigating the alleged acts of corruption and any other type of crime in the bidding processes and concession agreements, including their execution during the 2011-16 government period (government of former president Ollanta Humala Tasso), referred to Line 2 and Branch of Ave. Faucett, Ave. Gambeta, of the basic network of the Metro of Lima and Callao, of the concession agreement of the project, Improvement of the Energy Security of the country, Development of the South Peruvian Gas Pipeline, and of the contracts for the exploitation of Camisea Gas and the Talara Refinery; whose objectives were to determine the alleged irregular events within the normal functioning and management of public affairs. For its investigation and report, the Investigating Commission requested two reports from Osinergmin and invited it to the session in order to give a presentation on topics related to the investigation.
- Special Multiparty Commission in charge of Investigating the Alleged Bribes and Illegal Benefits that public officials of the different levels of government had received, in relation to the concessions, works and projects that have been awarded to the Brazilian companies Odebrecht, Camargo Correa, OAS, Andrade Gutiérrez, Queiroz Galvao and others, from the beginning of their activities to date by any form of contracting with the Peruvian State; whose lines of action are to identify Peruvian companies that, in joint ventures with Brazilian companies, participated and/or participate in bidding processes with the Peruvian State, signing contracts and modifications that may have meant or mean harmful acts to the State; to determine the alleged bribes and illegal benefits that public officials who intervened in the cases investigated have received; establishing functional and political, administrative and/or criminal responsibilities, among others.

These commissions, through an extension on their term, continue to be active in this 2017 – 2018 Annual Session Period, except for the first one that concluded its report, which was approved by the members of the Commission and is waiting to be brought to debate and taken to vote, for approval or rejection, in the Plenary Session of the Congress.

More generally, according to article 96 of the Political Constitution of Peru, any representative of the Congress may request the Government bodies and the Administration in general, all the information they deem necessary, carrying out the request in writing and in accordance with the Regulations of the Congress, causing legal liabilities in case of lack of response.

The First Vice-Presidency of the Congress of the Republic is responsible for overseeing the compliance of public entities and carries out its annual balance. Also, quarterly compliance reports are prepared and submitted to the Presidency of the Ministers Cabinet for evaluation.

During the 2011-16 parliamentary period, the Congress made an average of 226 requests for Information per annual session period. These include requests from congressmen and/or ordinary or investigating commissions. This number increased in 2016-17 and decreased in 2017-18 (see Table 2.17)

Table 2.17. Requests for information and opinion by Congress per parliamentary period

Parliamentary period	Number of requests for information	Number of requests for opinion
2011-12	174	45
2012-13	207	22
2013-14	245	29
2014-15	250	24
2015-16	255	15
2016-17	287	44
2017-18	173	27

Note: Periods run from August to July each year.
Source: Information provided by Osinergmin, 2018.

There is a procedure to answer requests by the Congress of the Republic (PI31, approved in November 2013) that defines response deadlines to the areas involved in order to meet the response deadline established by the Congress itself. A system keeps a record of all the entries from the Congress in order to follow-up the response, within the term established by the Service Procedure.

Another type of information request is the Request for Opinion on a specific bill that an ordinary commissions or a congressman requests as part of a commission so that a technical report by from Osinergmin provides feedback to the opinion on the bill prepared by said commission. During the 2011-16 parliamentary period Congress made an average of 27 Requests for Opinion per annual session period. In the current parliamentary period, which includes the 2016-17 and 2017-18 (until April) annual session period, the Congress has made an average of 36 annual Requests for Opinion.

Output and outcome

Measuring and assessing the performance of regulated entities

Osinergmin collects a vast amount of data from regulated entities across the energy and mining sectors. The majority of the data collected feeds into regulatory and supervision processes. In some cases, Osinergmin departments use the data to measure and report the performance of regulated sectors. The annual report (*Memoria Institucional*) presents a selection of performance indicators. Sector-specific reports and bulletins provide more in-depth information on each market and, in some cases, carry out an assessment of future needs. For example, indicators tracking capacity and natural gas processing plants are used to assess the need to expand and modernise infrastructure as well as maintenance schedules.

However, a holistic, organisation-wide approach to both data management and performance monitoring is lacking. The following paragraphs provide more detail on Osinergmin's current approach to data management and performance reporting, including some recent notable advancements.

Data collection requirements vary across sectors and industries. With respect to infrastructure supervision, Osinergmin tracks the number of accidents, incidents, injuries and fatalities. These figures are reported on a monthly basis in the hydrocarbon and mining sectors. Data is used to rank facilities based on their level of risk and hence prioritise supervisions. The regulator also publishes those statistics online and streams live statistics on TV screens across the offices, drawing attention of the staff operating in those sectors. With respect to service quality, regulated companies in the electricity sector must submit monthly reports on the quality of service. Street lighting statistics are instead collected twice a year.

Operators do not generally perceive the data requests from Osinergmin to be too onerous. However, the different authorities with some responsibility for sector regulation (MEM, Osinergmin, OEFA, and SUNAFIL) tend to make several data requests at the same time, making it difficult for companies to reply on time. Osinergmin often receives data after the deadline and some companies have not complied with data obligations in the past. Against non-compliance, Osinergmin usually sets up meetings with the company in question to discuss potential issues and improve future communication. The regulator can also initiate sanctioning procedures.

Most statistics are presented nationally. In some cases, Osinergmin uses some of the data collected to analyse and report on the performance of regulated sectors. For instance, in the electricity sector, the privately-owned companies operating in and around Lima have a much stronger performance compared to the public companies operating in the regions. Private companies tend to have better technical and financial means to achieve higher efficiency and quality of service; they also benefit from lower marginal costs. Conversely public companies face very strict borrowing constraints that reduce their ability to invest in innovation. Similarly in the mining sector, safety and performance issues are typically local in nature. Several extractive activities are currently on hold due to *force majeure* episodes. These mainly involve local protests and blockades resulting from the local residents opposing large-scale infrastructure projects. Both issues point to the need to continue monitoring performance at the sub-national level.

The analysis of performance that emerges from the wealth and breadth of data collected by Osinergmin does not systematically lead to remedial action to tackle the issues identified. The use of capacity data in natural gas processing plants described above is an example of monitoring based on regular data feeds. Another notable initiative is the collaboration between Osinergmin and the public electricity distribution companies under the National Fund for Financing Public Enterprise Activity (FONAFE). Since 2012, the regulator holds regular working group with those ten companies in order to tackle issues of service quality in the regions, especially around interruptions to electric services caused by disconnections in the infrastructure they operate. These meetings have resulted in detailed action plans that Osinergmin monitors in order to evaluate progress and prepare follow-up actions. In parallel, Osinergmin is involved in monitoring problems associated with operational conflicts in facilities at the border of different jurisdictions.

Osinergmin also uses some performance data as input for regulatory activities such as tariff-setting and benchmarking. For example, since 2015, tariff setting for the electricity distribution charges includes an adjustment factor to promote improvements in the quality of service (see Box 2.6).

A number of ongoing initiatives aim at strengthening data collection and use practices. The recently created Energy and Mining Observatory (OEM) represents a sizeable step forward in the provision of integrated, accessible data and analysis for the electricity, hydrocarbons and mining sectors. The OEM supports regulatory and supervisory processes and can be freely accessed both by the regulated companies and the wider public. In addition, a Data Warehouse is being developed (using the Agile methodology) to provide all employees with comprehensive information and unbiased access to data.

Box 2.6. Using performance data across regulatory functions

Performance measures also feed directly into the economic regulation functions of Osinergmin. The process of setting electricity distribution tariffs takes into account the Distribution Added Value (DAV). The DAV is the remuneration each electricity distribution company is allowed to attain considering investment, operation and maintenance costs of providing distribution services.

Since 2015, the definition and methodology for accounting for the DAV includes an adjustment factor to promote improvements in the quality of service. The adjustment factors are applied as an incentive or penalty on the compliance with annual goals. The latest modifications of this adjustment factor included a requirement that the quality of supply should be evaluated based on global performance indicators related to interruptions:

- Average Interruption Frequency per user (SAIFI)
- Average Total Time (in hours) of Interruption per user (SAIDI)

The methodology for the calculation of the SAIFI and the SAIDI of an electric system within a certain period is defined in the "Procedure for the Supervision of the Operation of the Electric Systems", approved by Board of Directors Resolution No. 074-2004-OS/CD. Both indicators provide a measure of the extent to which supply is affected by interruptions caused by failures, manoeuvres and unavailability in the generation, transmission or distribution electrical installations.

The adjustment factor that acts as an incentive above the DAV is granted at the beginning of the tariff period (1 November each year), and cannot exceed more than 5% of the DAV. The adjustment factor that acts as a penalty corresponds to the refund of the additional income granted following the DAV tariff setting process.

The introduction of these two indicators for the evaluation of the quality of the electric service provided by each distribution company is a very important step forward in linking performance evaluation and tariff-setting.

Source: Information provided by Osinergmin.

Last, Osinergmin collects data on the number of fines and sanctions administered – and appealed – as well as the number of user complaints collected – and addressed. These figures appear in annual reports and are communicated to other entities (e.g. Osinergmin shares data on user complaints with Indecopi) but the regulator does not explicitly include them among performance measures.

Assessing the performance of the regulator

Osinergmin assesses its performance through a variety of instruments that evaluate the regulator's ability to deliver its strategic objectives, the satisfaction and expectations of its employees, the regulator's reputation among stakeholders and their satisfaction with Osinergmin's processes and decisions.

Measuring Osinergmin's performance requires a balanced assessment of both the performance of the regulated entities and the performance of the regulator itself. This is a challenging task given the different markets that Osinergmin supervises and regulates, as reflected in the regulator's organisational structure. The large number of strategic goals adds additional complexity to the monitoring of outputs.

Osinergmin's strategic framework is based on the overarching Strategic Institutional Plan 2014-2021 (PEI) which sets out 15 strategic objectives based on four perspectives: stakeholders; internal processes; human sources development, learning and technology; and financial resources. This is accompanied with 40 strategic initiatives and 30 indicators (the full breakdown of the PEI can be found in Annex 2.A).

Every year, Osinergmin produces a detailed report (*Evaluación del Plan Estratégico 2015-21*) monitoring the timeliness with which the strategic initiatives are being implemented. The report, prepared by the GPPM under the supervision of the General Manager, includes quantitative indicators about the number of initiatives completed (15 in 2014, 11 in 2015 and 14 in 2016) out of those that were planned. The overall objective is to implement all the 40 strategic initiatives by 2021.

However, the report does not follow up specifically on the quantitative indicator laid out in the PEI. For example, the credibility, trust, autonomy and transparency indices are not regularly reported on with follow up actions. Instead, the report presents the overall results for the Global Reputation Index of Osinergmin. In 2016, the Index had a score of 641 out of 1 000. In addition, the report includes a comprehensive description of the action taken across all Departments to meet the goals of each specific strategic initiative.

In parallel, at the beginning of the year Osinergmin produces a Strategic Operational Plan (POI) which assigns direct responsibilities and budgets to the various Departments. The plan is devised on a 3-year basis, as is the budget, but it is updated annually to reflect changing circumstances. The overall POI is evaluated quarterly and the Policy and Economic Analysis Department (GPPM) produces the monthly performance assessments that are submitted to the Board. Each year, Osinergmin must also report indirectly on the POI by sending the underlying financial data to MEF. In addition, the PCM and Congress request a presentation of indicators. The OCI also produces an audit of the POI. Hence the financial performance of Osinergmin is assessed externally by different government bodies, using different indicators.

Osinergmin uses the budget execution indicator to measure its effectiveness in terms of its use of financial resources and this is also used to prepare the next planning phase. Osinergmin´s budgetary process involves the stages of: programming, formulation, approval, execution, and budgetary evaluation. At the beginning of each planning period, all Departments set out the resources needed to fulfill their functions. In parallel, GPAE forecasts the energy and mining industry revenues in order to calculate the rates of regulatory contributions for the next three-year period. After that, GPPM assesses the available budget for the coming year(s). During execution, when deviations from historical spending occur in any given Department, such Department needs to justify the increase or decrease and the impact on the process indicators that they are in charge of. In 2015 and 2016, over 90% of the budget was executed; in 2017, the figure declined below 80%.

Besides figures on the performance of the regulated sector, Osinergmin's Annual Reports also contain some assessment of the regulator's performance. For instance, worker satisfaction is tracked through bi-annual surveys "Great Place to Work". Overall satisfaction reached a 10-year high in 2017 with a 75% satisfaction rate, compared to 71% in 2015 and 68% in 2013. A very large share of employees felt "pride" of working at Osinergmin, whereas a below-average number of employees identified with "respect" and "impartiality". Osinergmin also monitors staff turnover which has been stable around 16% between 2015 and 2017. However the turnover among permanent staff is much lower at around 3-5%.

Last, Osinergmin collects data on the number of fines and sanctions administered – and appealed – as well as the number of user complaints collected – and addressed. These figures appear in annual reports and are communicated to other entities (e.g. Osinergmin shares data on user complaints with Indecopi) but the regulator does not explicitly include them among performance measures.

Notes

[1] Hydrocarbons Transport Regulation, approved by Supreme Decree No. 081-2007-EM, and the Natural Gas Pipelines Distribution Regulation, whose Single Unified Text was approved by Supreme Decree N ° 040-2008-EM, contains provisions related to access to infrastructure.

[2] The free market conditions are established the "Procedure to set the conditions of use access free to the Electric Transmission and Distribution Systems", approved by Resolution of the Osinergmin Board No. 091-2003-OS/CD.

[3] See article 10 of Law No. 27588, Framework Law on Regulatory Agencies for Private Investment in Public Utilities.

[4] After Value Added Tax (VAT) and Municipal Promotion Taxes.

[5] "*Administrative Service Contracting*" (*Contratos Administrativos de Servicios*, CAS).

[6] Law No. 28212, in accordance with Supreme Decree No. 046-2006-PCM, approved new remuneration caps for the public sector. Emergency Decree 038-2006, which modified Law 28121, reduced the remuneration for the President and Managers of regulatory bodies.

[7] Osinergmin's Board of Directors approved regulations related to safety measures for GLP cylinders following a full Regulatory Impact Assessment.

References

OECD (2016), *OECD Public Governance Reviews: Peru: Integrated Governance for Inclusive Growth*, OECD Public Governance Reviews, OECD Publishing, Paris, https://dx.doi.org/10.1787/9789264265172-en. [2]

OECD (2016), *Regulatory Policy in Peru: Assembling the Framework for Regulatory Quality*, OECD Reviews of Regulatory Reform, OECD Publishing, Paris, http://dx.doi.org/10.1787/9789264260054-en. [1]

Annex 2.A. Strategic Plan and Indicators

Objective	Description	Indicator
G1. Achieve credibility and trust of the society in the role of Osinergmin	The main objective that Osinergmin must seek in its new context is to maintain its legitimacy through the satisfaction of its relevant groups, as well as the credibility and trust of society. This legitimacy will allow our country to generate consistent investments in the energy, hydrocarbon and mining sectors.	Credibility index GPAE is responsible, and produced annually Trust index GPAE is responsible, and produced annually
G2. Develop rules and processes, with autonomy, transparency and predictability for the business sector	As the action of the regulator happens in the context of power and influence relationships between the public, political, social entities and of media, its strategic challenge is to maintain its autonomy. In this context, the transparency and predictability of regulations in the power, hydrocarbon and mining sectors must be ensured, in order to generate stability and an improvement in the degree of competition, thus preventing the decision-making process from being unduly influenced.	Autonomy index GPAE is responsible, and produced annually Transparency index GPAE is responsible, and produced annually
G3. Promote the improvement of coverage at the national level of sufficient, affordable and quality services	It is of utmost importance for the energy sector to be able to meet energy needs, essential for the productive activities of the country, identifying in advance the requirements associated with economic growth, and promoting access and efficient use of energy; as well as maintaining the mining development of Peru. In addition, new markets must be developed and poles of development created, so that growth is not slowed down.	Level of electricity coverage in the queues (ordered by geography) GFE & GOP is responsible, and is produced semi-annually Change in the Single Distribution Tariff by Tariff Category GFGN & GART is responsible, and is produced annually Sectoral index of the quality of service GPAE is responsible, and is produced quarterly
G4. Serve the requirements of stakeholders in an understandable, quick and efficient form	The interest of consumers is the ultimate goal of any process of economic regulation and supervision. Consumers, particularly domestic consumers and especially the most vulnerable, need simple, understandable and precise information about their rights and the behaviour of operators, price comparison facilities, procedures and means to present their complaints and claims. Osinergmin is particularly obliged to fulfill a task of consumer training and defence of their interests	Index of understanding OC Departments are responsible, and is produced annually Index of compliance with the statistical information system targeting each interest group OS is responsible, and is produced semi-annually
G5. Encourage that the operations of the companies are safe for the community, workers and the environment	Osinergmin must supervise compliance with legal and technical provisions in energy and mining activities, including those related to infrastructure security, its facilities, security management and operations, in order to anticipate and limit any negative consequence derived from said activities.	Frequency index of fatal accidents GFM, GFE, GFGN, GFHL, GOP are responsible, and produced monthly
P1. Integrate and improve the regulation, supervision and audit processes	By definition, supervision and regulation are the essential functions of Osinergmin, and improvements in exercising its functions should be the core of both the objectives and lines of action of Osinergmin for the coming years. In the case of the supervisory function, it is necessary to	Regulatory processes improved GART is responsible, and is produced annually Supervision processes improved *Sistema Integrado de Gestión* is responsible, and is produced annually

Objective	Description	Indicator
	incorporate a preventive approach that anticipates any possible problem in the activities of the regulated sectors. In the area of regulation, a comprehensive review of the regulatory framework is necessary in order to update, harmonise and give consistency to the standards.	Oversight and sanctioning processes improved *Sistema Integrado de Gestión* is responsible, and is produced annually Index of progress in the integration plan of regulation, supervision and oversight processes (actions / initiatives) OPC is responsible, and is produced quarterly
P2. Incorporate a long-term global vision in energy and mining that promotes the development of initiatives for a sustainable industry policy	It is necessary to incorporate a long-term vision of the regulatory and supervisory functions of Osinergmin, so that the performance of the regulator is part of a long-term sustainable sector policy, with an integral, transversal, multidisciplinary and inter-agency approach that contributes to the definition of the strategic position of the sector, oriented toward the society and the citizen.	Proposals to assess risk to energy supply and risk to mining operations GFE, GFGN, GFHL, GFM are responsible, and produced annually Security of Supply Index (SoS) GPAE, GART, Supervision Department are responsible, and is produced annually
P3. Promote decentralisation and linkage processes between consumers and companies	It is necessary to adapt the energy services to the realities and needs of the different areas of the country, seeking that citizens can count on the benefits of energy according to their needs and the context in which they live, enabling the improvement of their quality of life. In this context, Osinergmin is in the process of decentralising its functions and having an active national presence.	Index of the process of decentralisation GOP is responsible, and is produced semi-annually Provincial cases that are reviewed in Lima GOP is responsible, and is produced annually
P4. Strengthen communications with stakeholders	Osinergmin as a regulating and monitoring entity for energy and mining, requires a comprehensive communication strategy that meets the dual objective of making internal information flows more efficient and, on the other hand, making the results of its management visible to all stakeholders of the power, hydrocarbon and mining sectors.	CRM implementation progress in OSINERGMIN GOP and OC are responsible, and is produced quarterly
P5. Develop the conditions for regional energy interconnection	One of the trends identified during the development of the strategic plan is that Latin America will follow the development of other energy markets, especially in relation to the interconnections between countries at the level of electricity and natural gas. In this context, Osinergmin will develop an active role in regional gas and electricity initiatives, determining access conditions, connection fees, the use of national resources and their parameters.	Index of completion of prospective studies in energy and mining sectors OPC is responsible, and is produced semi-annually
P6. Monitoring and regulating investment commitments in new infrastructure	Regarding investments in new infrastructure in the energy, hydrocarbon and mining sectors, Osinergmin's actions must include the supervision and regulation of the project portfolio, thus ensuring the sustainable and secure development of these sectors.	Actual investment / Committed investment GG is responsible, and is produced semi-annually Remuneration of assets GART is responsible, and is produced semi-annually
D1. Develop innovation and creativity through organisational learning and knowledge management	The challenge for Osinergmin is to develop a culture that is not only open to innovation, but that actively encourages it.	Number of proposed regulation and supervision methods GART, GFHL, GFGN, GFE, GFM are responsible, and is produced annually Index of the implementation of the Knowledge System GTH is responsible, and is produced semi-annually
D2. Build an attractive organisation through the professional and personal development of its employees	Osinergmin must work in the development of an attractive and challenging work environment that promotes professional and personal development, and in the development of the service culture in favour of external and internal users.	Index of satisfaction with the work environment GTH is responsible, and is produced annually Index of the implementation of a career growth plan

Objective	Description	Indicator
	Talent management should focus on the redesign of the performance evaluation model that allows the identification of talent; achieving greater staff motivation.	GTH is responsible, and is produced monthly Index of progress in the implementation of the professional development plan GTH is responsible, and is produced monthly Index of progress in the implementation of the personal development plan GTH is responsible, and is produced monthly
D3. Have adequate information systems and technologies that provide support to OSINERGMIN's activities	Osinergmin must have information systems that allow it to adapt to continuous changes in the environment, technological advances, and changes in citizens' preferences.	Number of innovation projects under the Strategic Plan for IT OS Departments are responsible, and is produced semi-annually
F1. Use the budget efficiently	It is necessary to have mechanisms to be able to account for the actions of Osinergmin and monitor the use of funds available for the performance of the work entrusted.	Average cost per supervised entity OAF is responsible, and is produced monthly

Notes: The letters correspond to the four main perspectives: stakeholders (G); internal processes (P); human sources development, learning and technology (D); and financial resources (F).
Source: Material provided by Osinergmin, 2018.

Annex 2.B. Perception Survey of Regulated Companies

Osinergmin distributes the *Survey of Perception of Regulated and Supervised Companies* (EPERS) survey to regulated entities annually, which seeks to measure their perceptions of Osinergmin.

The EPERS survey of firms in the regulated sectors and other stakeholders, such as Congress, includes a question on their satisfaction with the services provided by Osinergmin. The questions ask for opinion on aspects such as trust, impartiality, transparency, predictability of decisions and quality of services provided. It also solicits the opinion of the regulated entities on the way in which Osinergmin carries out supervision activities and other duties. See below a summary of the categories of questions asked by the EPERS survey for the hydrocarbon and mining sectors.

Annex Table 2.B.1. Summary of categories of questions asked in the EPERS survey

	Hydrocarbons	Mining
Population surveyed	• Upstream companies (exploration and exploitation) • Downstream companies (consumers, transportation, service points i.e. gas stations, and ____)	• Medium and large mining companies operating in the national market
Population size	1 914	• 100 units – 82 belonging to metallic mining, and 18 to non-metallic mining
Sampling method	• Upstream: Census, due to small sample frame • Downstream: Stratified random sample	• Census, due to the small sample size
Total number of data points reported on	167	66
Main indicators examined	1. Characteristics of units surveyed o Units responding o Turnover of units in the industry o Profile of units responding the survey 2. Evolution of the perception of Osinergmin 3. General perception of Osinergmin o Perception index o Knowledge of Osinergmin o Opinion of various aspects of Osinergmin, including level of agreement/disagreement with Osinergmin as reliable, impartial, credible, independent, and transparent o Management by Osinergmin of sub-sector o Comparison of Osinergmin to other supervisory entities o Methods and appropriateness of communicating with Osinergmin o Opinions of the web portal, including relevancy of information	1. Characteristics of units surveyed o Units responding o Turnover of units in the industry o Profile of units responding the survey 2. General perception of Osinergmin o Perception index o Knowledge of Osinergmin o Opinion of various aspects of Osinergmin, including level of agreement/disagreement with Osinergmin as reliable, impartial, credible, independent, and transparent o Management by Osinergmin of sub-sector o Methods and appropriateness of communicating with Osinergmin 3. Perception of the Mining Supervision Department (GSM) o Similar categories as above o Opinions on media and communications channels to transmit information to entities

Hydrocarbons	Mining
o Opinions on the supervision process, including its contribution to improving company's processes, combating informality, clarity and usefulness of procedures, etc. o Opinions of PRICE system o Opinions of the sanctioning process o Satisfaction with the information request process 4. Perception of the Division for the Supervision of Hydrocarbons (DSHL) o Similar categories as above 5. Perception of the supervisory and sanctioning processes	o Opinions of the web portal, including relevancy of information 4. Evaluation of the supervision and sanctioning processes o Opinions on the supervision process, including its contribution to improving company's processes and usefulness of procedures, etc. o Opinions of GSM as a supervisory authority o Opinions of the sanctioning process, including how it can be improved o Satisfaction with the information request process 5. Comparison of Osinergmin to other regulatory entities

Source: EPERS reports for Liquid Hydrocarbons and Mining, 2016.

Annex A. Methodology

Measuring regulatory performance is challenging, starting with defining what to measure, dealing with confounding factors, attributing outcomes to interventions and coping with the lack of data and information. This chapter describes the methodology developed by the OECD to help regulators address these challenges through a Performance Assessment Framework for Economic Regulators (PAFER), which informs this review. The chapter first presents some of the work conducted by the OECD on measuring regulatory performance. It then describes the key features of the PAFER and presents a typology of performance indicators to measure input, process, output and outcome. It finally provides an overview of the approach and practical steps undertaken for developing this review.

Analytical framework

The analytical framework that informs this review draws on the work conducted by the OECD on measuring regulatory performance and the governance of economic regulators. OECD countries and regulators have recognised the need for measuring regulatory performance. Information on regulatory performance is necessary to better target scarce resources and to improve the overall performance of regulatory policies and regulators. However, measuring regulatory performance can prove challenging. Some of these challenges include:

- *What to measure*: evaluation systems require an assessment of how inputs have influenced outputs and outcomes. In the case of regulatory policy, the inputs can focus on: i) overall programmes intended to promote a systemic improvement of regulatory quality; ii) the application of specific practices intended to improve regulation, or, iii) changes in the design of specific regulations.
- *Confounding factors*: there is a myriad of contingent issues that have an impact on the outcomes in society which regulation is intended to affect. These issues can be as simple as a change in the weather, or as complicated as the last financial crisis. Accordingly, it is difficult to establish a direct causal relationship between the adoption of better regulation practices and specific improvements to the welfare outcomes that are sought in the economy.
- *Lack of data and information*: countries tend to lack data and methodologies to identify whether regulatory practices are being undertaken correctly and what impact these practices may be having on the real economy.

The OECD (2014[1]) *Framework for Regulatory Policy Evaluation* starts addressing these challenges through an input-process-output-outcome logic, which breaks down the regulatory process into a sequence of discrete steps. The input-process-output-outcome logic is flexible and can be applied both to evaluate practices to improve regulatory policy in general, and also to evaluate regulatory policy in specific sectors, based on the identification of relevant strategic objectives. It can be tailored to economic regulators by taking into consideration the conditions that support the performance of economic regulators (Box A A.1.).

The *OECD Best Practice Principles for Regulatory Policy: The Governance of Regulators* (OECD, 2014[2]) identifies some of the conditions that support the performance of economic regulators. They recognise the importance of assessing how a regulator is directed, controlled, resourced and held to account, in order to improve the overall effectiveness of regulators and promote growth and investment, including by supporting competition. Moreover, they acknowledge the positive impact of the regulator's own internal process on outcomes (i.e. how the regulator manages resources and what processes the regulator puts in place to regulate a given sector or market) (Figure A A.1).

Box A A.1. The input-process-output-outcome logic sequence

- Step I. Input: indicators include for example the budget and staff of the regulatory oversight body.
- Step II. Process: indicators assess whether formal requirements for good regulatory practices are in place. This includes requirements for objective setting, consultation, evidence-based analysis, administrative simplification, risk assessments and aligning regulatory changes internationally.
- Step III. Output: indicators provide information on whether the good regulatory practices have actually been implemented.
- Step IV. Impact of design on outcome (also referred to as intermediate outcome): indicators assess whether good regulatory practices contributed to an improvement in the quality of regulations. It therefore attempts to make a causal link between the design of regulatory policy and outcomes.
- Step V. Strategic outcomes: indicators assess whether the desired outcomes of regulatory policy have been achieved, both in terms of regulatory quality and in terms of regulatory outcomes.

Source: (OECD, 2014[12])

Figure A A.1. The OECD Best Practice Principles on the Governance of Regulators

Source: Adapted from (OECD, 2014[2]).

The two frameworks are brought together into a Performance Assessment Framework for Economic Regulators that structures the drivers of performance along the input-process-output-outcome framework (Table A A.1).

Table A A.1. Criteria for assessing regulators' own performance framework

References	Strategic objectives	Input	Process	Output and outcome
Best Practice Principles for the Governance of Regulators	• Role clarity	• Funding	• Maintaining trust and preventing undue influence • Decision making and governing body structure • Accountability and transparency • Engagement	• Performance evaluation
Institutional, organisational and monitoring drivers?	• Objectives and targets • Functions and powers	• Budgeting and financial management • Human resources management	• Strategy, leadership and co-ordination • Institutional structure • Management systems and operating processes • Relations and interfaces with Government bodies, regulated entities and other key stakeholders • Regulatory management tools	• Performance standards and indicators • Performance processes and reports • Feedback or outside evidence on performance

Source: OECD Analysis.

Performance indicators

For regulators, performance indicators need to fit the purpose of performance assessment, which is a systematic, analytical evaluation of the regulator's activities, with the purpose of seeking reliability and usability of the regulator's activities. Performance assessment is neither an audit, which judges how employees and managers complete their mission, nor a control, which puts emphasis on compliance with standards (OECD, 2004[3]).

Accordingly, performance indicators need to assess the efficient and effective use of a regulator's inputs, the quality of regulatory processes, and identify outputs and some direct outcomes that can be attributed to the regulator's interventions. Wider outcomes should serve as a "watchtower", which provides the information the regulator can use to identify problem areas, orient decisions and identify priorities (Figure A A.2).

Figure A A.2. Input-process-output-outcome framework for performance indicators

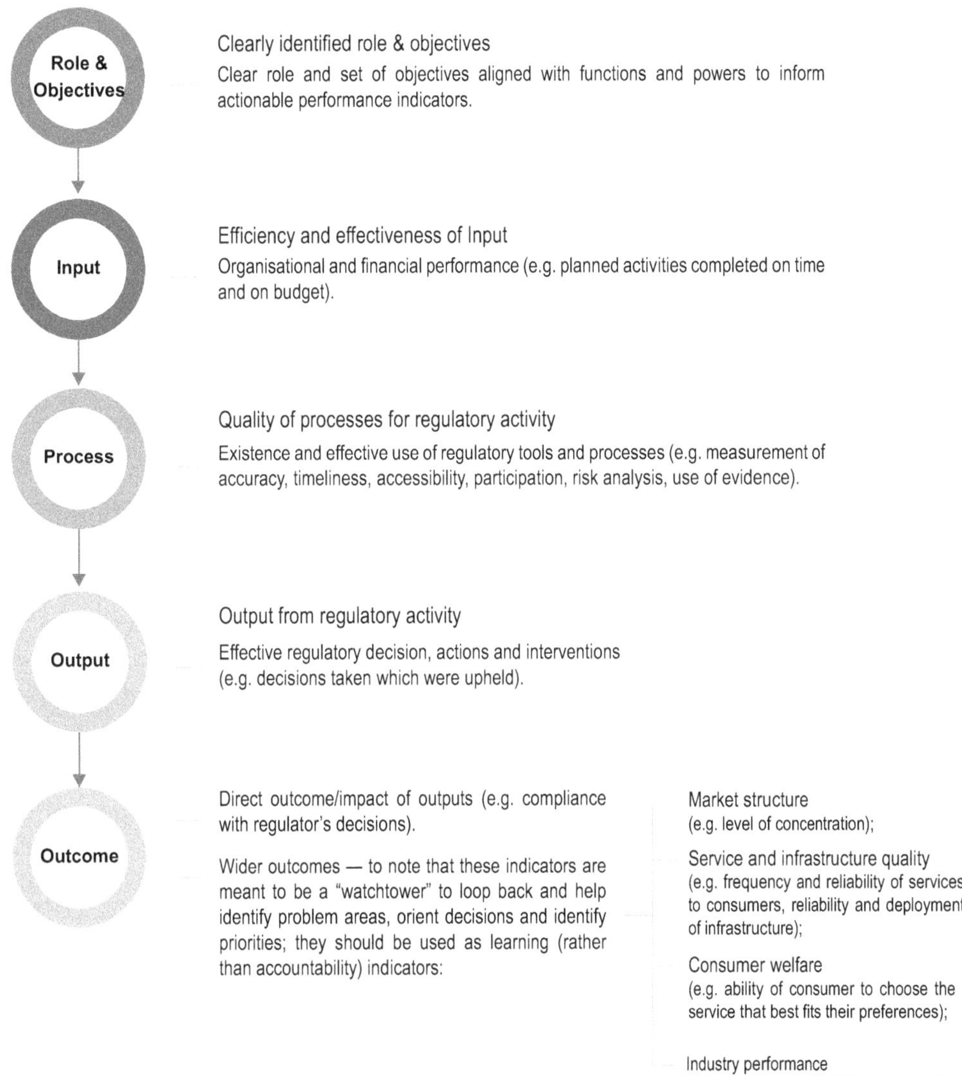

Note: This framework was proposed in the initial methodology for the performance assessment framework for economic regulators (PAFER) discussed with the OECD Network of Economic Regulators (NER). It has been refined to reflect feedback from NER members and the experience of other regulators in assessing their own performance.
Source: (OECD, 2015[4]), Figure 3.3 (updated in 2017).

Approach

The analytical framework presented above informed the data collection and the analysis presented in the report. The present report looks at the internal and external governance arrangements of Peru's Energy and Mining Regulator (*Organismo Supervisor de la Inversión en Energía y Minería*, Osinergmin) in the following areas:

- ***Strategic objectives***: to identify the existence of a set of clearly identified objectives, targets, or goals that are aligned with the regulator's functions and powers, which can inform the development of actionable performance indicators;
- ***Input***: to determine the extent to which the regulator's funding and staffing are aligned with the regulator's objectives, targets or goals, and the regulator's ability to manage financial and human resources autonomously and effectively;
- ***Process***: to assess the extent to which processes and the organisational management support the regulator's performance;
- ***Output and outcome***: to identify the existence of a systematic assessment of the performance of the regulated entities, the impact of the regulator's decisions and activities, and the extent to which these measurements are used appropriately.

Data informing the analysis presented in the report was collected via a desk review, a fact-finding mission and a peer mission to Peru:

- ***Questionnaire and desk review***: Osinergmin completed a detailed questionnaire which informed a desk review by the OECD Secretariat. The Secretariat reviewed existing legislation and OSIPTEL documents to collect information on the *de jure* functioning of the regulator, and to inform the basis of the fact-finding mission. This questionnaire was tailored to OSIPTEL, based on the methodology already applied by the OECD to Colombia's Communications Regulation commission (OECD, 2015[4])), Latvia's Public Utilities Commission ((OECD, 2016[5])), Mexico's three energy regulators (OECD, 2017[6]); (OECD, 2017[7]); (OECD, 2017[8]); (OECD, 2017[9]) and Ireland's Commission for Regulation of Utilities (OECD, 2018[10]).
- ***Fact-finding mission***: the mission was conducted by the OECD Secretariat on 25-28 June 2018 in Lima and was the key tool to collect and complete the *de jure* information obtained through the questionnaire with the *de facto* state of play. The work of the fact-finding mission tailored the PAFER methodology to Osinergmin features. Information collected was completed and checked with Osinergmin for accuracy, and issues for further discussion were also flagged.
- ***Peer mission***: the mission took place on 11-14 September 2018 in Lima and included peer reviewers in addition to OECD Secretariat. This mission took place concurrently with the peer mission for the PAFER review of Peru's Supervisory Agency for Investment in Telecommunications (*Organismo Supervisor de Inversión Privada en Telecomunicaciones*, OSIPTEL), which helped the peer mission team understand the systemic issues facing regulatory authorities in Peru. This mission met with key stakeholders in Osinergmin as well as externally. At the end of the mission, the team discussed preliminary findings and recommendations jointly with senior management from Osinergmin and OSIPTEL to test their feasibility and goodness of fit.

During the fact-finding and peer missions, the team met with Osinergmin's leadership team as well as a number of staff from across the institution, other government institutions and external stakeholders, including:

- National Institute for the Defense of Competition and Intellectual Property (*Instituto Nacional de Defensa de la Competencia y Protección de la Propiedad Intelectual*, Indecopi)
- Ministry of Economy and Finance (*Ministerio de Economía y Finanzas*, MEF)
- Ministry of Energy and Mines (Ministerio de Energía y Minas)
- Presidency of the Council of Ministers (*Presidencia del Consejo de Ministros*, PCM)
- Environmental Protection Agency (*Organismo de Evaluación y Fiscalización Ambiental*, OEFA)
- Peruvian Association of Consumers and Users (*Asociación Peruana de Consumidores y Usuarios*, ASPEC)
- Peruvian Organisation of Consumers and Users (*Organismo Peruano de Consumidores y Usuarios*, OPECU)
- Association for the Promotion of National Infrastructure (*Asociación para el Fomento de la Infraestructura Nacional*, AFIN)
- Journalists
- National Society of Mining Petroleum and Energy (*Sociedad Nacional de Minería, Petróleo y Energía*, SNMPE)
- Economic Operating Committee of the National Interconnected System (Comité de Operación Económica del Sistema Interconectado Nacional, COES)
- Sociedad Minera Cerro Verde S.A.
- Peru's Gas Transport Company (*Transportadora de Gas del Perú S.A., TGP*)
- Naturgy Energy Group S.A.
- Peruvian Society of Environmental Law (Sociedad Peruana de Derecho Ambiental)

References

OECD (2018), *Driving Performance at Ireland's Commission for Regulation of Utilities*, The Governance of Regulators, OECD Publishing, Paris, https://dx.doi.org/10.1787/9789264190061-en. [10]

OECD (2017), *Driving Performance at Mexico's Agency for Safety, Energy and Environment*, The Governance of Regulators, OECD Publishing, Paris, https://dx.doi.org/10.1787/9789264280458-en. [9]

OECD (2017), *Driving Performance at Mexico's Energy Regulatory Commission*, The Governance of Regulators, OECD Publishing, Paris, https://dx.doi.org/10.1787/9789264280830-en. [7]

OECD (2017), *Driving Performance at Mexico's National Hydrocarbons Commission*, The Governance of Regulators, OECD Publishing, Paris, https://dx.doi.org/10.1787/9789264280748-en. [8]

OECD (2017), *Driving Performance of Mexico's Energy Regulators*, The Governance of Regulators, OECD Publishing, Paris, https://dx.doi.org/10.1787/9789264267848-en. [6]

OECD (2016), *Driving Performance at Latvia's Public Utilities Commission*, The Governance of Regulators, OECD Publishing, Paris, https://dx.doi.org/10.1787/9789264257962-en. [5]

OECD (2015), *Driving Performance at Colombia's Communications Regulator*, OECD Publishing, Paris, https://dx.doi.org/10.1787/9789264232945-en. [4]

OECD (2014), *OECD Framework for Regulatory Policy Evaluation*, OECD Publishing, Paris, https://dx.doi.org/10.1787/9789264214453-en. [1]

OECD (2014), *The Governance of Regulators*, OECD Best Practice Principles for Regulatory Policy, OECD Publishing, Paris, https://dx.doi.org/10.1787/9789264209015-en. [2]

OECD (2004), *The choice of tools for enhancing policy impact: Evaluation and review*, OECD, Paris, http://www.oecd.org/officialdocuments/publicdisplaydocumentpdf/?cote=gov/pgc(2004)4&doclanguage=en (accessed on 16 November 2018). [3]

ORGANISATION FOR ECONOMIC CO-OPERATION AND DEVELOPMENT

The OECD is a unique forum where governments work together to address the economic, social and environmental challenges of globalisation. The OECD is also at the forefront of efforts to understand and to help governments respond to new developments and concerns, such as corporate governance, the information economy and the challenges of an ageing population. The Organisation provides a setting where governments can compare policy experiences, seek answers to common problems, identify good practice and work to co-ordinate domestic and international policies.

The OECD member countries are: Australia, Austria, Belgium, Canada, Chile, the Czech Republic, Denmark, Estonia, Finland, France, Germany, Greece, Hungary, Iceland, Ireland, Israel, Italy, Japan, Korea, Latvia, Lithuania, Luxembourg, Mexico, the Netherlands, New Zealand, Norway, Poland, Portugal, the Slovak Republic, Slovenia, Spain, Sweden, Switzerland, Turkey, the United Kingdom and the United States. The European Union takes part in the work of the OECD.

OECD Publishing disseminates widely the results of the Organisation's statistics gathering and research on economic, social and environmental issues, as well as the conventions, guidelines and standards agreed by its members.

OECD PUBLISHING, 2, rue André-Pascal, 75775 PARIS CEDEX 16
(42 2018 57 1 P) ISBN 978-92-64-31085-8 – 2019

www.ingramcontent.com/pod-product-compliance
Lightning Source LLC
LaVergne TN
LVHW081408110826
845149LV00010B/1667

9789264310858